BANNED
Baseball's Blacklist of All-Stars and Also-Rans

HAL BOCK

DIVERSIONBOOKS

Diversion Books
A Division of Diversion Publishing Corp.
443 Park Avenue South, Suite 1008
New York, New York 10016
www.DiversionBooks.com

For more information, email info@diversionbooks.com
All photographs courtesy of The Associated Press (www.apimages.com)

First Diversion Books edition February 2017.
Print ISBN: 978-1-63576-031-6
eBook ISBN: 978-1-63576-030-9

For Fran, As All Things Are
My Love,
My Life,
My Everything

Contents

Introduction

Hal Bock has chosen a subject of enduring fascination. Most of those banned from baseball over the years have been minor figures and, except for antiquarians, are shrouded in the mists of time. Other, more formidable players, prompt us — even decades after their deaths — to ponder the frailty of man, shake our heads and think what might have been.

Players, managers, umpires and executives have been banned from baseball ever since the first game-fixing incident in 1865. Prior to the onset of the Commissioner system in 1920, major league players were banned for a variety of offenses. The threat of blacklist was used as a cudgel to suppress player movement, to tamp down salary demands, and to punish players for drunkenness, insubordination, abuse of umpires, game fixing, obscenity and unsavory associations. The first game-fixing scandal and ensuing permanent expulsion (ultimately lifted in the case of each of the three New York Mutuals players banned:

Ed Duffy, William Wansley, and Thomas Devyr) date to 1865, eleven years before the launch of what we today term Major League Baseball.

Allegations of game fixing were rampant in the so-called amateur era and in the National Association, the professional circuit that in 1871–1875 preceded the National League. Bill Craver, later to be banished by the National League, was expelled by his Troy club for throwing games in 1871; however, he was signed by Baltimore. In 1874 John Radcliffe was expelled by the Philadelphia Athletics but nonetheless was picked up by the notoriously corrupt New York Mutuals. Two other players expelled in this year, Bill Boyd and Bill Stearns, were likewise "rehabilitated" for play with other clubs. This scenario played itself out similarly in the cases of Dick Higham, George Zettlein, and Fred Treacey in 1875, as each player was booted from one club only to land on his feet with another. In short, club suspensions or bans held no force in a climate of weak league control.

The first National League player (and thus the first in MLB history) to be expelled was George Bechtel in 1876. Banned by Louisville for game fixing, he too continued as an active player with the New York Mutuals for a few games until the NL stepped in. A game-fixing scandal in the following year nearly spelled the demise of the league and resulted in four players expelled for life, not only by their club but by the league (Jim Devlin, George Hall, Bill Craver and Al Nichols, all of Louisville). NL President William Hulbert declared the ban and never lifted it, despite appeals for reinstatement by some of the players and their supporters. These men were compelled to play in leagues not connected with the NL, sometimes under false names (a pattern continued by banned players in the 20th century).

In the years that followed many players were blacklisted or suspended indefinitely — which amounted to expulsion, as the end of the "sentence" was not in sight — either by their clubs or by a committee of the league's owners. In 1881–1882 the NL blacklisted ten players for a variety of offenses (mostly "lushing"), yet when a new rival major league, the American Association, declined to honor the NL bans and proceeded to woo the affected players, the blacklist was removed. In March 1882, the AA set a maximum penalty for drunkenness, insubordination and dishonorable or disreputable conduct: suspension for the balance of the season, plus the entire following season. Other offenses, however, might result in permanent ineligibility.

In the years leading up to the introduction of the Commissioner System in 1920 with the appointment of Judge Kenesaw Mountain Landis, indefinite suspensions, overt and covert blacklists, and definitive expulsions were common — more so in the years before the peace agreement of 1903 (the "National Agreement") than before. In that year baseball established a three-person National Commission (American League president, National League president, and a chairperson) to deal with issues affecting both major leagues, including the enactment and enforcement of fines and suspensions. Ban Johnson represented the AL during this time, while five NL presidents served. Garry Herrmann, president of the Cincinnati Reds and a lifelong friend of Johnson, was the chairperson for all 17 years of the National Commission's operation; critics thus accused Johnson of undue control over the game.

Johnson's failure to prevail in the Carl Mays case, in which the New York Yankees overturned his ruling in the courts, spelled the end of the National Commission. Also beset by troubling rumors concerning the 1919 World Series, the owners, seeking a single firm hand to guide the game through a rough patch, disbanded the National Commission and hired Landis, a seated federal judge.

The phrase "permanently ineligible" may have had its origin in a Landis ruling of 1926 in the Cobb-Speaker-Wood case, in which pitcher Hub Leonard had accused the three of conspiring to fix a regular-season series between Boston and Detroit in late 1919. Landis offered these guidelines for punishments going forward, clearly looking to disassociate his term in office from the myriad messes of yore. Much of this language is reflected in MLB's current Rule 21.

> *One — A statute of limitations with respect to alleged baseball offenses, as in our state and national statutes with regard to criminal offenses.*
>
> *Two — Ineligibility for one year for offering or giving any gift or reward by the players or management of one club to the players or management of another club for services rendered or supposed to be have been rendered, in defeating a competing club.*
>
> *Three — Ineligibility for one year for betting any sum whatsoever upon any ball game in connection with which the bettor had no duty to perform.*
>
> *Four — Permanent ineligibility for betting any sum*

whatsoever upon any ball game in connection with which the bettor has any duty to perform.

There are tales to be told — of Joe Jackson and Pete Rose and Dickie Kerr and more — and not without sympathy, but the person to tell those tales is the author. Read on!

—John Thorn, Official Historian
of Major League Baseball

—

Preface

"The integrity of the game is everything."

Peter Ueberroth, baseball's sixth commissioner, proclaimed that sentiment while serving in the position from 1984–1989. Though in the office for a short time, he clearly understood the essence of the sport and summed it up with just one sentence.

That credo captures the essence of all eight men who have served as baseball commissioner, from Judge Kenesaw Mountain Landis, hired in 1920, to Rob Manfred, who took office in 2015.

Their job is to protect the sport from those who would damage it, whether it's Landis dealing with gamblers and those who fixed games for bribes or Manfred addressing those who sought a competitive advantage by using steroids and other performance-enhancing drugs.

Judge Landis swept the game clean, starting with the eight Chicago White Sox players who were involved in the conspiracy to fix the 1919 World Series. The Black Sox players were found not guilty in court but guilty by Judge Landis. He reached the same conclusion when another star, Benny Kauff, was cleared of being involved in a stolen car ring but still thrown out of baseball by Landis. If you balked at signing a contract, the Landis solution was a suspension, sometimes for a year or two, sometimes for a lifetime. If you bet on games, the sentence was the same. And he kept right on suspending players who he thought threatened the basic structure of the game. The decisions did not always seem fair, but they were consistent.

Bowie Kuhn, who ruled the game for 15 years, saw danger when Hall of Famers Mickey Mantle and Willie Mays signed on as goodwill ambassadors for a pair of Atlantic City casinos and suspended the two icons. Some would argue that Kuhn went too far when all Mantle and Mays were doing was playing golf and glad handing customers. Ueberroth thought their jobs were rather benign and reinstated the two stars.

Happy Chandler sat Leo Durocher down for a year because he didn't like the company the manager was keeping and when a fistful of players succumbed to big money offers to play in Mexico, Chandler suspended them, too.

Perhaps the most dramatic suspension was the lifetime ban Bart Giamatti issued to Pete Rose, baseball's hit king. There was evidence that Rose had bet on games, sometimes his own, and Giamatti had no choice but to discipline him. The case drained Giamatti, and he died just eight days after handing down the suspension. His successors, Fay Vincent, Bud Selig and Rob Manfred, saw no reason to reinstate Rose.

This biography looks at the history of such baseball

suspensions and how they impacted the game from the Deadball Era right up to the present. It includes a list of the players who have been banned and the language of baseball rules that were violated. Each time the commissioner acted, it was because he believed the future of the game itself was at stake *and* moved to protect it.

Almost always, the decisions spurred debate. Sometimes they were viewed as too harsh, sometimes too lenient. In every case, though, Peter Ueberroth's observation seemed to hold the answer.

"The integrity of the game is everything."

CHAPTER 1

The First Four — and More

When baseball first surfaced as an organized sport, it was populated by an underclass of individuals — transients and vagrants, drunkards and miscreants, the underbelly of society. They were a ragtag crew of characters, fond of gambling and carousing, not exactly a group you would invite to your next cocktail party.

No one was more offended by this unseemly congregation than William Hulbert, a prosperous Midwestern businessman who found himself in 1875 as president of the National Association's Chicago White Stockings. As distressed as he was by the questionable character of the players, Hulbert was just as annoyed by Boston's domination of the league. So he raided the Red Stockings, luring pitcher Albert Spalding and three other players to Chicago. And then, fearing retribution by his National Association partners, Hulbert staged a first strike, creating his own league for his newly fortified Chicago franchise. In February 1876, the National League was born with eight teams, including the Louisville Grays.

The new venture came with some strict rules of behavior — no drinking, no gambling and no games on Sundays. The old method of doing business was out. Hulbert was resolute. His new league would be squeaky clean. This approach created a problem in Louisville.

The Grays had been a middle-of-the-pack team in the National League's first season, finishing in fifth place, a fat 22 games behind Hulbert's champion White Stockings. Louisville's star pitcher was Jim Devlin, who had a record of 30-35, a 1.56 earned run average and led the league with 122 strikeouts. But there was a bit of a black cloud during their season when outfielder George Bechtel was nailed for fixing games and tossed from the team. Among the players he approached was Devlin, who turned down the proposal but would eventually drift to the dark side anyway. Bechtel hooked up with the New York Mutuals for a couple of games before Hulbert caught on and barred him for good, making him the first player thumbed out of baseball for life. His misdeeds planted a seed in Louisville, and it blossomed the next year.

In 1877, Louisville shot to the top of the league, compiling a 27-13 record and opening a four-game lead when the Grays embarked on a tumultuous August road trip. They would lose 10 of the next 11 games, some of them under suspicious circumstances. The downward spiral began with a 6-1 loss at Boston, a game in which Devlin, a decent hitting pitcher, struck out four times. Then came a 5-1 loss to Hartford, followed by a 7-0 shutout against Hartford.

In three games, the Grays had been outscored 18-2. They started the trip losing and kept right on doing that. The string of losses was interrupted only by a 1-1 tie against Hartford and a 3-2 victory over Cincinnati. Otherwise, the road trip was a drumbeat of loss after loss.

Louisville's lead evaporated quickly, consumed in an avalanche of errors and misplays. Most of the losses weren't close and before long, the Grays fell 6 ½ games behind. Suddenly Devlin, perhaps the most consistent pitcher in the league, had become woefully ineffective. The plunge ended when the Grays completed the trip by losing three of four games at Cincinnati, a visit that produced the only Louisville win after eight straight losses on the journey.

Watching all this was John A. Haldeman, a baseball writer for the Louisville Courier Journal, whose father, Walter Haldeman, happened to be president and part owner of the team. The younger Haldeman became suspicious as the Grays stumbled through the road trip and tumbled into second place. Louisville managed a meager 21 runs in the 11 games, never more than three in any game. Meanwhile, Devlin suddenly became very hittable, allowing fewer than five runs just four times during the trip.

There were hints everywhere that something unscrupulous was going on. Included were some mysterious telegrams to a club official before a pair of games against Hartford, suggesting the fix was in. Louisville lost both games with Devlin pitching poorly and costly errors by George Hall and Al Nichols playing a key role. Devlin abandoned his best pitch, the equivalent of a modern-day sinker. Hall, who hit .323 for the season, managed just four hits in the 11 games. There were also a host of telegrams to the players that raised suspicions. Something clearly was up — "funny business" was the way John Haldeman described it — and the questions built when Devlin suddenly regained his effectiveness as Louisville won seven of its last nine games. The Grays fell short, though, finishing seven games behind Boston, which won 20 of its last 21 games, including four against Louisville. Haldeman wrote about the strange sequence of events almost every day.

Finally, club officials called Devlin in for a meeting, and the pitcher denied any wrongdoing. He was outraged at the suggestion that he had done anything wrong. Hall, however, was unnerved by his teammate being summoned by the front office and thought the pitcher had confessed. That led Hall to admit what was going on and he implicated Nichols, who, Hall said, was the go-between for the players and the gamblers. A fourth player, Bill Craver, was also implicated after refusing to divulge the contents of telegrams sent to him. Craver came to the Grays with some baggage after being kicked off the Chicago White Stockings in 1870 for cavorting with gamblers.

Eventually, Devlin admitted his involvement, claiming Hall and Nichols had approached him with a $100 offer to throw an exhibition game. After that, he said, he was pulled into the larger scheme. Further complicating the landscape was the report that umpire Dan Devinney had been offered $250 to ensure that Louisville lost an August game against St. Louis. He may have been targeted because of all the umpires who worked Louisville games, the Grays won more times when Devinney was officiating than they did with any of the others.

Soon, the whole mess found its way to Hulbert, who

came down hard on the quartet of Louisville players. The league president was outraged and cracked down on the situation, assembling a blacklist of players suspected of bad behavior. Most were eventually reinstated, but two, Eddie "The Only" Nolan and Lip Pike, were banned for life. No one, however, was more devastated by the turn of events than Devlin. He pitched every inning of every game for the Grays that season, and now he was thrown out of baseball.

The following winter, the pitcher made his way to Chicago for a face-to-face meeting with Hulbert to plea for another chance. Hulbert was having none of it. As far as he was concerned, the pitcher had violated one of the new league's most sacred tenets. Fixing games was a cardinal sin, and Devlin and his three teammates would pay a severe price.

Albert Spalding was in the next room during the meeting and reported the raw emotions that surfaced between the disgraced pitcher and the National League president.

Devlin had tears in his eyes as he pleaded for a second chance. He dropped to his knees, sobbing over what this punishment would do, not only to him but to his family. His wife and child would suffer, he said. Hulbert, too, grew emotional. He had feelings for the player but greater ones for the integrity of baseball. The league president reached into his pocket, pulled out a $50 bill and pressed it into Devlin's hand.

"That's what I think of you personally," he said to the pitcher, "but damn you Devlin, you are dishonest. You have sold a game and I can't trust you. Now go and let me never see your face again for your act will never be condoned as long as I live."

The expulsion of the four Louisville players led the Grays to disband and drop out of the league. Also leaving was the St. Louis franchise, which had a deal with Devlin for the following season and suddenly was left without one of the league's premier pitchers. With baseball no longer an option, Devlin needed a new profession, and the centerpiece of the Louisville Grays fix found an ironic one. He embraced a career of law and order, becoming a police officer.

CHAPTER 2

Lipman Pike and the 1881 Blacklist

Lipman Pike was baseball's first genuine slugger.

Evidence for this comes from his statistics. He once hit six home runs in a game — although some accounts say it was only five — and led the old National Association in home runs three times. In 1871, his first season, he led the league with four home runs and 21 extra base hits. The next year, he led the league with seven homers and 60 runs batted in. In 1874, he had 22 doubles and a .504 slugging percentage, leading the league in both categories. These were big numbers for a small man who stood only 5 foot 8 and weighed just 158 pounds.

All of this did not prevent Pike from being barred from baseball — twice. And it might have been three times, except no one showed up for a disciplinary hearing by the

National Association of Base Ball Players in 1871 when Pike was to be charged with accepting $20 a week to play for the Philadelphia Athletics, violating baseball's amateur rules. When no one appeared, the matter was forgotten. But William Hulbert didn't forget it.

Hulbert was a Chicago businessman who founded the National League in 1876, determined to sweep away the eclectic community of characters, not all of them upstanding citizens, who populated the National Association teams. His effort was only marginally successful, as evidenced by the need to ban four Louisville players for fixing games in 1877.

In 1881, Hulbert once again moved against players he found offensive. The National League blacklisted nine players, placing them under an umbrella of "general dissipation and insubordination." Lipman Pike led the players swept away by the blacklist broom, which included Mike Dorgan, Emil Gross, Perry "Sadie" Houck, Bill Crowley, John Fox, Blower Brown, Lewis "Buttercup" Dickerson and Eddie "The Only" Nolan. Each of them was believed to have stretched the boundaries of proper behavior, often with public intoxication, sometimes with adjusting the outcome of games.

Perhaps the most offensive to Hulbert were Pike, the pint-sized slugger, and Nolan, who by most measures was an ordinary pitcher. When the American Association refused to recognize the blacklist, Hulbert reinstated seven of the players. The bans on Pike and Nolan, however, were supposed to be permanent, although that didn't turn out to be the case.

Pike was something of a baseball vagabond. Dismissed

from Philadelphia because he was a New York native and thus a "foreigner" in baseball terms, he made stops playing in New Jersey with The Irvingtons, New York with The Mutuals and Brooklyn with The Atlantics. He was playing second base for the Atlantics when they ended Cincinnati's 93-game winning streak. When the National Association was formed in 1871, Pike moved to the Troy franchise and starred, leading the league with four home runs. He drifted then to Baltimore, where he led the league in homers each of the next two years.

Pike was a showman, something of a matinee idol with his bushy mustache and athletic prowess. And he was fast, often running match races against opponents for a cash prize. Perhaps his crowning match race achievement occurred in 1873, when he engaged in a 100-yard race with a harness horse named Clarence. Timed in 10 seconds, he won by 4 yards and took home the $250 purse, no small sum in those days.

There were stops in Hartford, Cincinnati — where he won his fourth home run title — and, by 1878, Providence. That season, he angered officials with an undisclosed misdemeanor and was sent packing. Pike sat out three seasons before surfacing again, this time with Worcester in 1881.

His time away from the game had taken a toll. Pike was 36 years old and batting just .111 when one September afternoon, he committed three errors in the ninth inning, giving Boston two runs in a 3-2 victory. He was accused of fixing the game, and three weeks later, he was blacklisted by the league — his second banishment. Included on the blacklist list that day were Mike Dorgan and Buttercup

Dickerson, who also happened to be playing for Worcester as teammates of Pike when the errors were committed.

Pike made one more cameo appearance six years later at age 42, went 0-for-4 and was finished with baseball, returning to the more serene activity of running a haberdashery business. Baseball did not forget him, though. In 1936, the first year of balloting for the Hall of Fame and 43 years after he died, Lipman Pike's career batting average of .322 and slugging average of .468 earned him one vote from the Veterans Committee. Someone remembered the little guy with the big bat.

Nolan was fond of liquid refreshment and found ways to be excused from his team in order to pursue that passion. In 1878, pitching for Indianapolis, he won 13 games but was suspended briefly for fixing a game. When he returned, he got in trouble again, this time for begging off a road trip to attend a family funeral. The fact that no one had died was just incidental. That episode led to another suspension, this one lasting. Nolan returned in 1881, just in time to be part of Hulbert's house cleaning.

His permanent suspension was ended after two years, but he might as well not have bothered returning. The Only Nolan won only two more games before ending his career.

There are two versions of an explanation for his unusual nickname. The first is that he was, in fact, baseball's only Nolan. The second is that he reminded observers of a burlesque character of the time who called himself "The Only Leon."

Even though The Only Nolan's lifetime Major League statistics were a modest 23-52, there is some evidence that he dominated in other settings. He is said to have won 64 games with 30 shutouts with an 0.50 earned run average in 1877 while pitching in the League Alliance. Statistics from that time are haphazard at best, but those numbers are startling. So, however, was his ability to get into trouble with the proprietors of the National League.

The other players swept away by Hulbert's blacklist broom were an intriguing group. Mike Dorgan was primarily a catcher, but he never bothered with a mask, instead using pieces of rubber to protect his teeth and mouth. He also doubled as Worcester's manager, and with the team buried in last place in 1881, he was suspected of throwing games. The same rumor doomed his teammate Lewis Dickerson, who had the engaging nickname of Buttercup.

Dickerson had as much affection for alcohol as Nolan did and was not shy about pursuing it. He also was fond of jumping teams, an annoying habit that led him from Cincinnati to Troy to Worcester to Pittsburgh to St. Louis to Baltimore and to Louisville in a career that lasted just seven years. Most of his moves came after he sat out one season because of the Hulbert blacklist. The suspension did not deter him from continuing to drink, and in one famous episode while playing for St. Louis, he disappeared in Baltimore for a couple of days and then showed up for a game playing for Baltimore against his old St. Louis team.

Emil Gross was one of baseball's best catchers — except when he had to actually catch. That was an issue. Gross had 291 hits in five seasons and 242 errors, a rather remarkable combination of statistics. His .295 career batting average was acceptable. His .895 fielding percentage was not.

Houck was a very good shortstop and hitter. In 1879, his rookie season with Boston, he was among the league's top 10 in extra base hits, doubles, triples and runs scored. He also was among the league leaders in liquid refreshment. By 1881, he was warned about his excessive drinking and blithely ignored the admonition. He went right along his merry way until Hulbert grew weary of his act and suspended him as well.

The nine men out included some of the era's best ballplayers, but Hulbert wanted to clean up baseball and acted swiftly and dramatically to achieve that goal. Unfortunately for him, the punishments were shrugged off, and when the players were reinstated, baseball continued to have alcohol and gambling issues right into the next century.

CHAPTER 3

This Ump Is "Outta Here!!"

Baseball umpires are a unique breed, the keepers of law and order on the field, required to make decisions, often almost in a split second, on every play. And when they do, somebody won't like it.

Was that a ball or a strike?

Was that runner safe or out?

Did the hitter swing or hold up?

Who instigated the beanball brawl?

An umpire's job is to apply the rulebook, a sometimes complicated set of regulations. Occasionally they make a mistake in that pursuit, and they are punished for the miscue. Sometimes they are suspended for a game or two. Sometimes the penalty is longer. Among umpires suspended recently for either misinterpreting the rules or making physical contact with a player were Fieldin Culbreth, Joe

West, Bob Davidson, Mike Winters, John Shulock, Tom Hallion and John Hirschbeck.

The game's best-known umpire was Bill Klem, who worked at baseball's most important job from 1905–1941. He offered a credo for the craft when he once said of a play, "It ain't nothin' till I call it."

Klem was baseball's most respected umpire. Others did not share that quality. There was, for example, James Johnstone, who was run off by Giants manager John McGraw in August 1906. Johnstone had called out Josh Devlin of the Giants on a close play at home plate in a game against the Chicago Cubs, and when the home team lost, fans rushed the umpire, who needed a police escort.

McGraw barred Johnstone from the Polo Grounds the next day, for his own safety, the manager said. Under the rules at the time, when one of the game's two umpires was unavailable, the home team designated a substitute. Sammy Strang, a Giants bench player, drew the assignment. Cubs manager Frank Chance was having none of that and refused to play. Strang declared a forfeit for the Giants, pleasing McGraw. Johnstone, stranded outside the park, declared a forfeit for the Cubs. National League president Harry Pulliam upheld Johnstone's ruling, awarding the forfeit to the Cubs. What's more, he ordered Johnstone right back to the Polo Grounds the next day. The umpire complied, perhaps with some trepidation, but was warmly received by the crowd. It was a step up the respect ladder for the profession.

The umpires do the best they can under often difficult circumstances, with fans howling at them and having a manager in their face, questioning a call, screaming obscenities, perhaps kicking dirt on them. The umpire's only recourse is to throw the complainer out of the game.

There was a time, however, when baseball threw the umpire out of the game.

Born in England in 1851, Dick Higham and his family moved to the United States before he was 3 years old, and he grew up to become a baseball player. He batted over .300 six times in an eight-year career that began in the National Association and ended in the National League. He led the NL in doubles in each of his last two years and compiled a career batting average of .307. In 1874, he managed the New York Mutuals, notorious for their shenanigans on and off the field, to a 29-11 record and a second place finish in the National Association, which decided the final standings on wins alone. For part of the next season, he was captain of the Chicago White Stockings but was discharged for associating with gamblers and fixing games. He also served as a part-time umpire in the National Association.

But he was getting a bad reputation. There were whispers about Higham, suggestions that he did not always do his best on the field, that he might have been involved with some unsavory characters who had an interest in the outcome of games. He committed some suspicious defensive lapses, causing some doubts about his dedication to the game. There were rumors about fixed games in July and August 1873 and June and August 1875. Higham played every position except pitcher and was charged with 323 errors for his career, raising some eyebrows. He was suspended at least twice.

Despite his shady reputation, Higham was hired in 1881 as a National League umpire. In a complicated arrangement, umpires were hired by team owners and then often were assigned to one team's games. In 1882, the National League decided to add umpires to its list of personnel required to stay away from gamblers. Higham drew 26 of Detroit's first 29 games that season and before too long, team owner William Thompson, the mayor of Detroit, became convinced that the umpire was doing business with hoodlums. Most of Higham's close calls were going against Detroit, and Thompson demanded an explanation. The team owner hired a private detective to watch the umpire, and before too long, he discovered letters between Higham and a known gambler that clearly implicated the umpire.

The two men had set up a telegram code. If Higham's telegram said, "Buy all the lumber you can," it meant to bet on Detroit. If there was no telegram, it meant to bet against Detroit.

Thompson and other owners confronted Higham, and halfway through his second season as an umpire, he was fired. He denied the accusations and never admitted to any wrongdoing, but two days after he was dismissed, Higham was banned from baseball. He remains the only umpire in history to be thrown out of the game permanently.

CHAPTER 4

The Good Umpire
and the Bad Doctor

Few pennant races have ended with the drama of the 1908 National League pennant chase. Three teams — the New York Giants, Pittsburgh Pirates and Chicago Cubs — were locked in a pulsating charge through September, separated in the standings by mere percentage points.

That's when Fred Merkle lost his way on the basepaths and Dr. Joseph Creamer lost his job as the Giants team physician.

Merkle's boner, failing to touch second base on what appeared to be the game-winning hit, caused a crucial game between the Giants and Cubs to be ruled a tie. When the teams ended the season deadlocked for the pennant, it forced a playoff game. That's when Dr. Creamer tried to fix the outcome.

The idea of one game to settle a season-long battle had New York in a frenzy. The bathtub shaped Polo Grounds, home of the Giants, was teeming with people as the two ball clubs arrived for the game. Crowds spilled into the streets surrounding the ballpark, fans frantic to watch this showdown match with winner-take-all implications. Some even scrambled up the elevated subway tracks outside the ballpark, and one unfortunate man, fireman Henry McBride, fell from the structure to his death. His place on the El quickly went to someone else.

Inside the ballpark, betting and gambling were rampant everywhere. This was 1908, when that activity was widespread. Adding to the drama was the fact that there was bad blood between the two teams. Before the game, Giants manager John McGraw kept his team on the field longer than usual, cutting into the Cubs' practice time. There were scuffles between the two teams, including one ugly one between Giants pitcher Joe McGinnity and Cubs manager Frank Chance.

That was nothing compared with what was going on in a hallway behind the field. It was there that Dr. Creamer, the Giants team physician, approached umpire Bill Klem with a proposition. He was carrying a fistful of money with him.

"Here's $2,500," the doctor said to the umpire. "It's yours if you will give all the close decisions to the Giants and see that they win for sure. You know what is behind me, and you needn't be afraid of anything. You will have a good job for the rest of your life."

That was a pretty good chunk of change in 1908, when the average American earned $600 a year and most baseball players made about $3,000. The highest paid player at the time was Nap Lajoie, a future Hall of Famer, who earned $8,500.

Dr. Creamer's words were ominous, but he had picked the wrong customer. Bill Klem was in his third year working in the National League, well on his way to establishing a reputation as baseball's finest umpire. In his career, he worked a record 18 World Series, called five no-hitters as a home plate umpire and developed hand signals for umpires as well as the smaller inside chest protector. He established a reputation as the best in the business at his craft. And he didn't get that way by participating in fixes.

Klem brushed off Creamer's proposal. The game would be played cleanly. But the umpire was not through with the doctor. He reported the bribery attempt to National League president Harry Pulliam, who launched an investigation.

Creamer denied the episode had ever happened. Klem swore that it had. Pulliam, a gentle soul with no stomach for this kind of controversy, believed his umpire and informed the Giants of his finding. The team then advised Dr. Creamer that he would no longer serve as their physician. And Pulliam took a stronger position, barring Dr. Creamer from baseball entirely. The doctor may be the only individual attached to a team in a peripheral role to be banned from baseball for life. But he had earned the sentence. Baseball was striving to clean up the environment at the time, and a bribe attempt was a black eye for a sport that was just beginning to gain its footing on the American sports landscape.

Years later, speculation began that Dr. Creamer had been a scapegoat and that the man who had set up the bribe attempt was McGraw. The Giants manager was a rough and tumble character, a racetrack regular who certainly was familiar with some disreputable characters. And he had a reputation for some unwholesome shenanigans. When he played third base for the Baltimore Orioles, he was fond of grabbing the belts of base runners to slow them down. He also succeeded in singlehandedly preventing the 1904 World Series from being played as a payback in a long-standing feud with American League president Ban Johnson. He once got into a disagreement with umpire Bill Byron and punched the ump in the face, a show of temper that earned him a $500 fine and 16-day suspension. He questioned the integrity of National League president John Tener, earning another $1,000 fine. McGraw certainly was a tough hombre. But bribing an umpire? Such a move would have endangered his reputation for life. For his part, Dr. Creamer never implicated the Giants manager. He simply denied making the overture to Klem.

Pulliam's ruling hardly scared off the gamblers. Betting remained an integral part of baseball's profile. The game was appealing to the underground because players were easy targets, perceived as underpaid and poorly treated by owners and often only too willing to fix the outcome of games in order to earn a few extra dollars. There were repeated instances of players being suspended, sometimes for a few games, sometimes for years, sometimes for life.

The Cubs won the playoff game that Dr. Creamer had tried to fix and went on to win the World Series, the last world championship for the franchise in more than 100 years until winning again in 2016. Bill Klem umpired for 33 more years and then took an administrative job as the head of National League umpires until his death in 1951. Dr. Creamer disappeared from baseball.

Harry Pulliam was shaken by the whole affair of 1908 — the Merkle decision, the need for a playoff game, the attempted bribe of an umpire. He fell into a deep depression and, in February 1909, suffered a nervous breakdown. It took him several months to recover, but that summer he returned to work. One day in July, he got up from dinner in the New York Athletic Club, where he resided, and returned to his room, where he pulled out a revolver and committed suicide.

CHAPTER 5

The Chalmers Chase

In the first decade of the 20th century, transportation in America was moving from a landscape dotted with horse-drawn carriages to a marvelous new invention called the motorcar. This remarkable machine played a central role in the 1910 American League batting race and the eventual banishment from baseball of John O'Connor, a manager with the engaging nickname of "Peach Pie" and one of the team's coach-scouts, Harry Howell, who was called "Handsome."

Among the early manufacturers of motorcars was the Chalmers Motor Company, which produced a spiffy-looking model that featured a zippy four-cylinder, 30-horsepower engine with an interior of vinyl upholstery. It was a head-turner, and Hugh Chalmers decided that the best way to advertise his new product was to award one to the baseball player with the season's highest batting average.

The National League's leading hitter that season was Sherry Magee at .331, far removed from the top averages in the American League, where two of the Deadball Era's best hitters, the mercurial Ty Cobb of the Detroit Tigers and Napoleon Lajoie of the Cleveland Indians, were engaged in an exciting showdown. Magee was unhappy that Chalmers wasn't awarding cars to each league's batting champion but sat back to watch two of the era's greatest hitters battle it out for the prize. Lajoie had assembled four straight batting championships from 1901–1904, while Cobb had won three straight beginning in 1906 and was on his way to 4,000 career hits. It would be a dandy battle.

The Chalmers challenge energized their 1910 season. Who would get to drive off in that fancy new car? An enterprising photographer posed the two stars in the open-top Chalmers auto, both looking determined to prevail. They were polar opposites: Lajoie easygoing and so well-liked that the Cleveland franchise took the name Naps to honor him, Cobb perhaps the most driven player in baseball history, who would do anything to win, often bending the rules of good sportsmanship.

Midway through the season, Lajoie seemed to have a lock on the Chalmers 30 car, soaring 30 points in front of Cobb, who was struggling with eye problems. But as the schedule turned into its final weeks, Cobb went on a tear and moved in front. It was then that Peach Pie O'Connor stepped into the battle.

O'Connor had been a major league catcher for 21 years, much of it in the middle of an era of baseball that was full of roughhouse tactics. The players were tough characters, not exactly high society sorts that you might invite to a cocktail party, and O'Connor fit right in. In 1910, he found himself managing the lowly St. Louis Browns, a terrible team on the road to nowhere. In O'Connor's one and only season as manager, the Browns finished 47-107, the second worst record in franchise history, a colossal 57 games out of first place.

Cobb went into the final weekend of the 1910 season batting .383, comfortably in front of Lajoie, who was at .376. Checking the numbers, Cobb decided to pass on the season's last two games, claiming his eyes were acting up again and protecting his average. Some observers thought he was faking it, especially when he headed for Philadelphia to play in a pre-World Series All-Star Game against the American League champion Athletics, a game designed to keep the A's sharp for the Series. Lajoie would need a boatload of hits to catch him. Peach Pie O'Connor decided to make sure Cobb's rival got them.

Cleveland had a doubleheader against St. Louis on the final day of the season. With nothing at stake for either team, O'Connor stepped into the Lajoie-Cobb fray. Before the game, he grabbed rookie third baseman Red Corriden and instructed the youngster to play deep, very deep, whenever Lajoie came to bat or else he might be knocked out by a line drive. With Corriden stationed on the lip of the outfield grass, the Browns were extending a gracious invitation to Lajoie to beat out bunts for base hits each time he came to the plate and fatten his batting average in his pursuit of Cobb. Corriden followed orders.

In his first at-bat of the doubleheader, Lajoie hit a ball to center field. Rookie Hub Northen went back a bit unsteadily, and the ball landed behind him for a triple.

Lajoie either hadn't noticed Corriden's positioning, or he didn't care. After that, though, he decided to accept the invitation to bunt. Six times, his eyes lit up like a pinball machine, and he dropped down bunts. Each time, he beat out the bunt for a hit, his batting average creeping a little higher with each hit. Every time Lajoie came to the plate, Corriden returned far behind third base, inviting another bunt. And every time, Lajoie obliged. On one of the bunts, shortstop Bobby Wallace fumbled the ball and was charged with an error by official scorer E.V. Parrish. And that's when O'Connor and Handsome Harry Howell really got into hot water.

Howell visited Parrish and asked if the scorer might consider changing the error to a hit. Nope, Parrish was sticking with his original ruling — error. Later, a batboy showed up with a pointed message for the official scorer. Change the error to a hit, and there would be a new suit of clothes in the bargain for doing the Browns and Lajoie that favor. Parish was having none of that scheme. The error stood, and Lajoie finished the day with eight hits — six of them bunt singles following his first at-bat triple — and a sacrifice in nine at-bats and a final batting average of .384, a fraction of a percentage point in front of Cobb. Or maybe it was behind Cobb. No one seemed quite sure. The last hit came in the ninth inning of the second game and was shrouded with questions because Lajoie made it to the plate only because the Browns issued a two-out walk and hit a batter. All the bunt hits left a cloud over Lajoie's numbers.

Statistics were kept in a rather haphazard fashion in those days, and no one could be certain if the final numbers — .3833992 for Cobb and .3840997 for Lajoie — were completely accurate. Some accounts gave the batting title to Lajoie, a development that led eight of Cobb's teammates to send a telegram to the Cleveland star, congratulating him on winning the championship. That's how much Cobb was disliked, even in his own clubhouse. "Cobb wasn't easy to get along with," said Sam Crawford, who played alongside him for 13 seasons in Detroit. "He came up with an antagonistic attitude."

Further complicating the issue was the delayed decision by official scorer Hugh Fullerton, who decided that a play in which he charged an error in an earlier game should be changed to a hit for Cobb, pushing him past Lajoie in the batting race. Chalmers wanted no part in this mess and solved it by awarding new cars to both players.

There was widespread outrage over the affair, described as "a deplorable spectacle" in one St. Louis newspaper. The matter quickly arrived at the doorstep of American League president Ban Johnson. When he heard what Peach Pie O'Connor and Handsome Harry Howell had done, he ordered both of them fired for their antics. At a time when there was considerable suspicion about widespread gambling and fixes in baseball, Johnson would not tolerate such shenanigans. Not only were O'Connor and Howell dismissed from their jobs with the Browns, but they were barred from baseball as well. Managers do not usually get permanent expulsions, but O'Connor had clearly earned his punishment.

The controversy did not end there. Years later, Sporting News researcher Paul McFarlane discovered that Cobb had been credited with two extra hits by a scoring mistake. Take away the hits, and Lajoie becomes the 1910 American

League batting champion. The matter landed in the lap of commissioner Bowie Kuhn, who decided 71 years after the Chalmers chase to leave the records intact, keeping Cobb as the 1910 season's leading hitter and maintaining the Hall of Famer's string of nine straight batting championships.

Official statistics, however, deducted the two hits from Cobb's career totals, dropping his record batting average from .367 to .366 and his hit total from 4,191 to 4,189. It hardly mattered to him, though, because the changes came long after he had died.

CHAPTER 6

Stealing Cars Instead of Bases

Benny Kauff was a baseball dandy, a flamboyant character who marched around like a flashing neon sign screaming, "Look at me! Look at me!" He was full of himself and never shy about sharing that opinion with anybody who would listen.

"I'll make them all forget Ty Cobb," Kauff once boasted, taking on the biggest star of his era. Truth be known, he backed up his boasts for a while, starring in the short-lived Federal League, which had been created to compete with the major leagues. He was dubbed the best player in the new league, dominating its statistics, first in Indianapolis and then in Brooklyn.

Kauff's first taste of the major leagues came in a five-game cameo stint with the New York Highlanders in 1912. After a year in Hartford, where he won the Eastern Association batting title with a .345 average, he was acquired by the St. Louis Cardinals, who sent him to the American Association's Indianapolis farm club, intending to park him there for future use. But the Federal League franchise in that city offered to double his salary, and Kauff felt no need to abide by his Cardinals contract and jumped to the new league. He led the Federal League in hitting the next two seasons, .370 in 1914, then .342 the next year. He also led the league in on-base percentage and stolen bases both seasons. He was the real deal.

But Kauff was also something of a shady character, and that led to an early exit from organized baseball. There were the contracts he ignored, the rumors of fixes that might have involved him and oh, yes, the stolen car affair that finally led to his banishment from the game.

Kauff was so impressed with his own performance in the first Federal League season that he decided he was a free agent and bailed out on his contract in 1915 to sign with John McGraw's New York Giants. That stunt was frowned upon, and when he tried to take the field for a game against Boston, the Braves protested, claiming Kauff was signed with the outlaw league. He was forced to remain in the Federal League, shuffled off to Brooklyn to satisfy an old debt by the Indianapolis club and was blacklisted by organized baseball. It was his first scrape with the proprietors of the game. It would not, however, be his last.

Kauff continued to dominate the Federal League in its second and final season, and when the Feds folded, he applied for reinstatement to Major League Baseball. It was granted, and he was back in spring training with the New York Giants the next season, arriving dressed like somebody straight out of Fifth Avenue's Easter Parade. He had a striped silk shirt, a tailored blue suit, patent leather shoes, a fur collared overcoat, all topped by a derby hat and walking stick. His accessories included a diamond stick pin, a diamond ring, a gold watch decorated with diamonds and a sizeable amount of walking-around cash. Benny Kauff was ready for the big leagues.

Attracted by the cozy fences at the Polo Grounds, he predicted great things for himself. There would be fistfuls of home runs, he said. He would beat a steady tattoo on the close-in walls. "They'll have to put up screens to protect the fans," he said. This, Benny Kauff promised, was going to be some show.

In his first year in New York, though, Kauff turned out to be rather ordinary, batting just .264, far removed from the fat numbers he put up in the Federal League. Some of his statistics were impressive — nine home runs, 15 triples, 40 stolen bases. Overall, however, he was good, but not great, as evidenced by his singular achievement in 1916 of being the only player in the 20thcentury to be picked off first base three times in one game. It turned out that Ty Cobb had nothing to worry about from Benny Kauff.

Kauff settled into a productive career with the Giants, consistently hitting over .300, even when his 1918 season was briefly interrupted by World War I service. He remained a dynamic character, though, always looking for some excitement. And soon, that was exactly what came his way.

With the Giants drifting through the 1919 season, teammates Hal Chase and Heinie Zimmerman decided to make some extra money by fixing games. They approached Kauff with their scheme, and he was outraged. At least he seemed to be. Contract jumping was one thing. But fixing games? No way. He went straight to McGraw to report what had happened. It was an attack of integrity that would have been impressive had it not been for some other behavior that suggested that Kauff was not exactly squeaky clean. There was the matter of the 1919 Black Sox scandal and rumors that Kauff played a role in the fixing of the World Series. At least, that's what Bill Maharg, one of the fixers said. And Arnold Rothstein, kingpin of the fix, claimed that Kauff had asked for $50,000 to help arrange the outcome of the Series.

So there was a cloud of suspicion over Kauff when, in the fall of 1919, he launched an auto parts business with his half-brother, Frank, and Giants teammate Jesse Barnes. It happened that in December, a car disappeared from a Manhattan parking lot and surfaced with a new paint job, new tires, a new license and a "For Sale" sign. A criminal complaint claimed that Kauff and two of his employees, James Shields and James Whelan, sold the stolen car for $1,800 to an unsuspecting customer, Ignatz Engel. Barnes was not implicated. What's more, the complaint added that the auto parts business was nothing more than a front for a stolen car ring. Kauff was outraged at the charge, claiming first that he had no idea the car was stolen and then that he was home having dinner with his wife at the time of the theft.

McGraw wanted no part of the scandal and traded Kauff to Toronto of the International League at the start of the 1920 season. Kauff blithely shrugged off the charges and flourished, batting .343 with 28 stolen bases before McGraw, noting the fancy statistics, reacquired him. The

Giants boss then served as judge and jury, stating, "Kauff is innocent of the charge of buying stolen automobiles. He simply got in with evil companions who mixed him into the case before he knew it."

The stolen car case went to trial on May 10, 1921. The jury bought Kauff's explanation that he had been duped by Shields and Whelan, who had shown him a phony bill of sale. The two ex-cons testified that Kauff was right in the middle of the stolen car scheme. The trial lasted four days, the deliberations lasted one hour and Kauff was acquitted — by the jury, but not by baseball.

Hired to clean up baseball after the Black Sox affair, Commissioner Kenesaw Mountain Landis was not amused by this affair. He had flexed his muscle with the lifetime ban of eight players involved in the Black Sox scandal and followed that by throwing out several other players for cavorting with suspicious characters. Gambling and fixing games were one thing, kind of run-of-the-mill felonies. A stolen car ring was, if nothing else, original in baseball circles. The commissioner had suspended Kauff, pending resolution of the criminal case, and then he decided to ignore the jury's verdict, which he thought was completely wrong.

"Benny Kauff's involvement in an auto theft ring smells to high heaven, and (his acquittal) was one of the worst miscarriages of justice ever to come to my attention," Landis said.

The commissioner wrote a scathing letter to Kauff, saying the trial had compromised the outfielder's character and reputation and that reinstating him would leave fans with serious questions about the integrity of the game. The commissioner told him he was no longer a fit companion for other players. That meant, Landis decided, Kauff was out for life.

The commissioner's decision seemed harsh, and Kauff tried to fight it, applying to New York State Supreme Court for a permanent injunction. But in January 1922, the court rejected Kauff's application. The Landis lifetime ban would stand. Benny Kauff's big league career was done after eight seasons, a career batting average of .311 and one stolen car scheme in which he was or wasn't really involved. Baseball was done with him, but he wasn't done with baseball. Kauff spent 22 years as a scout and then went into the clothing business, a perfect line of work for a man who always was attracted to stylish outfits.

CHAPTER 7

The Hal Chase Enigma

Those who saw him play always thought Hal Chase was one of the best fielding first basemen in history. Blessed with great speed that produced 363 stolen bases in 15 seasons, including 40 in one year, and terrific anticipation in the field, Chase was one of the defining stars of the Deadball Era.

So how come he committed so many errors?

Well, it may be because he is viewed as the most corrupt player of his time, always willing to operate on the shady side of the game until baseball got tired of his act and sent him packing. There is evidence that Chase offered bribes to fix games and took bribes to fix games. He was an equal opportunity miscreant, only too willing to operate outside the rules of the game.

Even though he was a defensive star, Chase managed to commit between 19 and 21 errors in six straight seasons and

402 over 15 seasons. Those are inordinately high numbers for someone lauded for his ability to play first base better than most players before or after him. He had a remarkable ability to look like he was trying, only to be failing. Sports writer Fred Lieb observed his act and decided Chase had "a corkscrew brain" because of his oddball approach to his craft. He could be a star in one inning or one game and then ruin things for his team in the blink of an eye.

He was an enigma.

Chase came out of California, where he played at Santa Clara University, claiming to have studied engineering there. The problem is there was never any evidence that he ever saw the inside of a classroom, and engineering was not part of the university's curriculum then anyway. Those were details. Chase was always a big picture guy.

His professional career began in the Pacific Coast League with the Los Angeles Angels, but by 1904, he was playing first base for the New York Highlanders, forerunners of the Yankees. His arrival in New York set off some unpleasantness between the two teams, a typical condition for Chase, who frequently found himself in the middle of squabbles. The Highlanders were the perfect spot for the first baseman. The team was owned by a couple of shady characters. Frank Farrell ran an illegal casino, and Bill Devery was a corrupt police captain and Tammany Hall official.

Chase immediately became a man about town, dazzled by the nightlife of the big city. He enjoyed seeing and being seen and quickly became a Broadway regular, embracing wine, women and song. He also wasted no time becoming involved in the culture of gambling and other nefarious business that permeated baseball at that time. The nightlife did not interfere with his production on the field. He was a solid hitter, a skilled baserunner and a defensive whiz — when he wanted to be. There were troubling lapses, though, that caused observers to wonder what was going on with the man called Prince Hal.

Four years into his stay with the Highlanders, Chase announced that he was jumping to the outlaw California League unless the team came up with a $4,000 contract. That was big money in those days, but Farrell and Devery agreed, whereupon Chase jumped to the California League anyway. Then he changed his mind and came back, having extorted the fat contract in the bargain. He often used the California retreat tactic to irritate teams he played for in the major leagues.

Chase consumed managers at a dizzying pace. The Highlanders went through six bench bosses, including Chase himself, who got the job after leaving the team in the middle of a trip and returning again to California, after demanding that George Stallings be fired. It was Stallings, after all, who had accused Chase of "laying down" on the team. It was the first time that charge was leveled at the first baseman. It would not, however, be the last. The new manager would be Hal Chase, who took the team from second place in 1910 under Stallings to sixth place in 1911 in his only year as manager.

Intrigued by the gambling environment of the times, Chase was an eager participant, readily admitting that he bet on games but never, he said, on those involving his own team. That, after all, wouldn't be right. Still, there were times when Chase mishandled routine chances and was late covering first base, brain-cramp plays that generally caused teammates and others to wonder just what was going on with him.

Chase's stay with the Highlanders ended in 1913 with a trade to the Chicago White Sox, prompted at least in part by suspicions that new manager Frank Chance — who knew something about playing the position — had about his first baseman. He concluded that Chase was throwing games and sent him packing. The White Sox kept him around for parts of two seasons, during which time he managed to commit 40 errors in 160 games.

Even though he was celebrated for his defense, Chase led the league in errors six times, never led the league in fielding percentage or putouts and, more than a century since his last American League game, still holds the AL record for errors by a first baseman (285), a mark he achieved in just 10 seasons. He still remained a commodity in baseball circles and had no trouble finding a home with Buffalo of the new Federal League. He flourished there, batting .347 after arriving in 1914 and then leading the league with 17 home runs the next year.

When the Federal League folded, Chase looked done. Rumors of his involvement with gamblers caused American League president Ban Johnson to bar him from returning to that league. But there was still the National League, a fertile new place to play. Chase surfaced with Cincinnati, where he led the league with 184 hits, a .339 batting average and just 14 errors in 142 games. But he was up to his old tricks after that, committing 41 errors over the next two seasons and catching the attention of manager Christy

Mathewson, who was baseball's best behaved citizen at a time when most of the game's participants were rogues.

Mathewson knew all about Chase's reputation for gambling, and when pitcher Jimmy Ring reported that the first baseman had approached him about fixing a game in August, the manager suspended Prince Hal for "indifferent play." It was the third time Chase's play had caused a manager to take action against him, following George Stallings and Frank Chance. Ring wanted no part of the fix, but when he lost the game anyway, Chase dropped $50 in his lap. When Mathewson suspended him, Chase was not prepared to take the punishment without a fight. He demanded to be paid and threatened to sue and drag baseball's good name through the mud. At a postseason hearing before National League president John Heydler, Ring's account could not be substantiated and Chase got off the hook.

The Reds had their fill of this unpleasantness and sent Chase to the New York Giants, where manager John McGraw delighted in trying to reform troubled players. And then, to add to the drama, McGraw hired Mathewson, returning from World War I service, to coach first base and keep an eye on the troubled Chase. The reclamation lasted until August, when widespread whispers implicated him and teammates Heinie Zimmerman and Lee Magee with approaching teammates about fixing games. It was an oft-told tale about Chase, and the Giants, like the Reds and White Sox and Yankees before them, gave up on the talented but troubled first baseman.

A few months after Chase was released, the Chicago White Sox conspired to fix the 1919 World Series against

Chase's old Cincinnati buddies. Chase was rumored to have some periphery involvement in the fix, but that charge was never proven. He returned to California, where he managed to be suspended from three different leagues for attempting to fix games.

Chase's life deteriorated from there. He became an alcoholic, drifting from job to job, often working for a night's lodging. When he died in 1947, the prince had turned into a pauper.

CHAPTER 8

A Chase To Nowhere

It wasn't that Heinie Zimmerman was a bad baseball player. In fact, he was pretty good. And it wasn't that he was a bad person. In fact, he was a standup guy, ready to defend himself whenever it became necessary. He just got in with a bad crowd, and bad things happened to him.

Zimmerman was a handy guy to have around a ball club, capable of playing second base, shortstop or third base. And he had a good bat with a .295 career batting average. How good a hitter was he? Well, there was, for example, the matter of the 1912 Triple Crown, which Zimmerman thought he had won when he led the league in batting (.372), home runs (14) and runs batted in (104). Another accounting, however, reduced his RBI total to 99. That meant no Triple Crown for Zimmerman until later research found the original number to be correct, restoring the achievement to the eccentric infielder.

Strange stuff like that made Zimmerman prone to mood swings on and off the field, and his baseball production reflected that. He was a combative character, often involved in brawls. Objecting to a call, he got into postgame fight with umpire Bill Finneran in 1912. A year later, he was thrown out of three games in five days, an impressive stretch of umpire baiting.

In one memorable clubhouse squabble, he hurled a bottle of ammonia that shattered in the face of teammate Jimmy Sheckard, nearly blinding the outfielder. When Frank Chance went after him in the aftermath of that episode, Zimmerman decked the manager, blackening both his eyes before teammates pulled him away. This was no way to win friends and influence people in your clubhouse.

Still, Zimmerman was the toast of Chicago in his Triple Crown year, but by 1916, the Cubs had tired of his up and down behavior and suspended him for his indifferent play. When the opportunity came to trade him, the Cubs made the deal, swapping Zimmerman to the New York Giants, where manager John McGraw delighted in importing reclamation projects who had struggled elsewhere.

Zimmerman actually flourished after the trade and led the league with 83 RBIs. The next season, 1917, he batted .295 and again led the league with 102 RBIs. He was doing well on the field but not so well away from it. He was keeping bad company, hanging around gamblers and a nefarious crowd. And that's why Zimmerman's performance in the World Series raised eyebrows. He batted just .120 and succeeded in chasing Eddie Collins across an unguarded home plate with the winning run of the Series in a tortoise vs. the hare foot race. Was he doing business in this futile foot race? Not this time. He became the goat of the Series because a couple of teammates butchered a simple play.

The controversial play began when Chicago's Happy Felsch hit a comebacker to Giants pitcher Rube Benton. When Collins broke for the plate, Benton threw the ball to Zimmerman and the rundown started. The much fleeter Collins sidestepped catcher Bill Rariden, and when Benton and first baseman Walter Holke both failed to cover home plate, the chase to nowhere was underway for Zimmerman. Collins slid home with the run that won the Series, and Zimmerman was left holding the bag and the baseball. As he noted afterward, the only person he could have thrown the ball to was home plate umpire Bill Klem.

After that, a malaise seemed to set in for Zimmerman. He often failed to hustle, and McGraw was forced to bench him for "indifferent play" when he failed to run out a pop fly. He often seemed distracted and disinterested.

And then, along came Hal Chase.

Acquired from Cincinnati as another one of McGraw's reclamation projects, Chase brought with him an unsavory reputation, rumors of doing frequent business with gamblers to fix the outcome of games. He quickly hooked up with Zimmerman, recruiting the infielder to join his unscrupulous activity. The two became fast friends, hanging out with a community of unsavory characters.

There were rumors everywhere about Chase and Zimmerman. Their reputations were well-known. By September, the rumors became facts when Zimmerman approached pitcher Fred Toney after the first inning of a game in Chicago, suggesting the pitcher let up on the

Cubs to make some extra money. Toney was having none of that and asked out of the game. Days later, Chase went after Rube Benton with a similar proposal. Benton won his game, and Zimmerman buttonholed him later with a message. "You poor fish," he said. "Don't you know there was $400 waiting for you to lose that game today?"

A few days later, Chase and Zimmerman approached Benny Kauff with another scheme, offering him $125 per game to control the outcomes. Kauff, hardly an upstanding character, turned them down but word filtered to McGraw of what the two players were doing. The manager suspended Zimmerman, allegedly for breaking curfew. What he had broken, though, was the faith of his manager and his team, something his buddy, Chase, had shattered before ever coming to the Giants.

When the Black Sox scandal rocked baseball following the 1919 World Series, eight players were indicted in the fix. At the ensuing grand jury hearings, McGraw implicated his two players. They had conspired with gamblers to fix games, and Chase was also said to have been involved peripherally in the Black Sox affair. The Chicago players were found innocent of the charges, but in the court of the new commissioner, Kenesaw Mountain Landis, they were guilty. Each of them was barred for life from organized baseball.

Zimmerman admitted to his actions in the grand jury hearings, claiming he was only doing a favor for a friend. He insisted his role in baseball's gambling crisis was nothing more than that of a messenger. Landis was unimpressed, and the commissioner's hammer came down again. The message from Landis was for Zimmerman to find some other line of work. He was blacklisted in 1919 in the wake of the Black Sox Series. The blacklist became a lifetime ban two years later. Zimmerman never again played organized baseball.

And by the way, neither did his sidekick, Hal Chase.

LEFT: The 1910 American League batting championship was won by Napoleon Lajoie and led to St. Louis manager Peach Pie O'Connor and Handsome Harry Howell being banned from baseball. (AP Photo)
RIGHT: The Black Sox scandal led to the appointment of Kenesaw Mountain Landis as baseball's first commissioner. (AP Photo)

LEFT: Star slugger Shoeless Joe Jackson was one of the Black Sox conspirators. (AP Photo)
RIGHT: Even though they were found not guilty, Commissioner Landis banned eight Black Sox players from baseball. (AP Photo)

CLOCKWISE FROM LEFT:

Giants manager John McGraw and umpire Bill Klem weren't exactly close pals. (AP Photo)

Fine fielding first baseman Hal Chase had a reputation for offering and accepting bribes to fix games. (AP Photo)

Fred Merkle's base running blunder led to a playoff game and when the Giants team physician tried to bribe umpire Bill Klem, the doctor was banned from baseball by Commissioner Landis. (AP Photo)

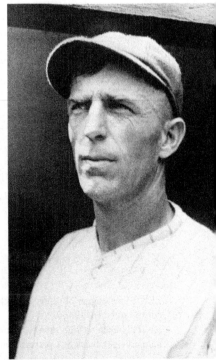

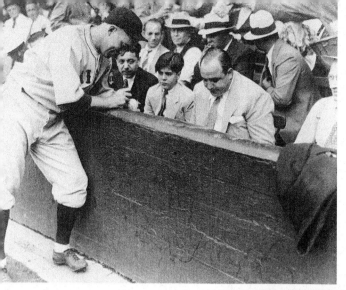

ABOVE: Cubs catcher Gabby Hartnett gets chummy with mobster Al Capone before a 1931 exhibition game in Chicago. (AP Photo)

RIGHT: Commissioner Landis cleaned up the game, often banning players for minor offenses. (AP Photo)

BELOW: Catcher Mickey Owen was used as a recruiter by Mexican League officials before he returned to the majors. (AP Photo)

LEFT: Happy Chandler was baseball's second commissioner and banned the Mexican League jumpers. (AP Photo)
RIGHT: Combative manager Leo Durocher was suspended for the 1947 season by Commissioner Happy Chandler. (AP Photo)

LEFT: Outfielder Danny Gardella was one of the first Major League players to leave for the Mexican League. (AP Photo)
RIGHT: Sal Maglie Jumped to the Mexican League and then when he returned to the majors became one of baseball's best pitchers, throwing a no-hitter for the Brooklyn Dodgers. (AP Photo)

CHAPTER 9

The Judge ... and the Jury

Baseball has often found itself in courtrooms and hearings, sued by players and fans and sometimes called on the carpet by the federal government. It was just that turn of events that led the game to its first commissioner, Judge Kenesaw Mountain Landis.

One of baseball's early legal dustups came against the upstart Federal League, which had pirated a number of players away from Major League Baseball and then, in 1914, sued to overturn the Reserve Clause, a restrictive bit of legislation that tied a player to his team in perpetuity. What's more, the Feds charged, Major League Baseball was a trust in violation of federal law.

The case landed in the lap of Landis, a federal judge in the Northern District of Illinois, who once fined Standard Oil a record $29,240,000, which happened to exceed that company's assets. That ruling was reversed on appeal, but it caught the eye of those interested in such legal matters. Landis also jailed anti-war activists during World War I and raised the ire of the American Bar Association, which initiated failed impeachment proceedings against the judge.

When he heard the Federal League suit quickly, it was expected that he would render a decision in short order. He did not, choosing to sit on the case, delaying long enough that the plaintiffs caved and settled. Major League Baseball was thrilled. The basic structure of the game had been saved. Landis was baseball's kind of judge.

The owners kept him in the back of their minds. You never know when a friendly judge could come in handy. And soon, Kenesaw Mountain Landis proved to be exactly that.

Baseball was brought to its knees by the scandal of the 1919 World Series, when members of the Chicago White Sox conspired with gamblers and lost the Series to the Cincinnati Reds. There had been rumors of a fix before and during the Series, and within a year, a grand jury was convened and eight players — Shoeless Joe Jackson, Eddie Cicotte, Lefty Williams, Chick Gandil, Buck Weaver, Fred McMullin, Happy Felsch and Swede Risberg — were indicted.

The trial in 1921 dragged baseball's name through the mud, and although the eight players were absolved of any wrongdoing, the sport was clearly in trouble with the American public. What baseball needed was a ruling body that would rebuild its reputation and maintain law and order. At the height of the Black Sox scandal, Major League Baseball owners — all of them except Philip de Cateby Ball of the St. Louis Browns, a contrary sort — visited Kenesaw Mountain Landis' Chicago courtroom and offered him a job as chairman of a three-man Board of Control over their industry. Landis didn't need the other two helpers. He demanded and received total control. Baseball had its first commissioner.

It didn't take long for Landis to demonstrate his approach to cleaning up the game. He noted the acquittal of the eight White Sox players implicated in the 1919 World Series scandal and promptly overturned it. The players might be innocent in the eyes of the court, but they were guilty in baseball's court, where Landis functioned as the judge and the jury. It was a tipoff to what his administration would be like. Baseball had hired a law and order judge to clean its house, and that's just what Landis went about doing. "Regardless of the outcome of juries," Landis said, "no player that throws a game, no player that sits in conference with a bunch of crooked players where the ways and means of throwing games are discussed and does not promptly tell his club about it, will ever again play professional baseball."

Further evidence that he was not concerned with findings of innocence in court came in the Benny Kauff case. When Kauff was implicated in a car theft ring, the case went to court, and the player was found innocent. Not in Landis' court, though. The commissioner barred Kauff for life.

He was sending a message. Baseball had a new sheriff, and he would be one tough hombre. Landis quickly nailed a fistful of other players. Jimmy O'Connell and coach Cozy Dolan of the New York Giants were sent packing following a failed bribe attempt. The commissioner did not like the company Philadelphia's Eugene Paulette was keeping and banned him. The same fate befell Joe Gedeon of the St. Louis Browns. When Lee Magee of the Chicago Cubs was released and sued for his salary, testimony implicated him in fixing games. Landis barred him for life, too. No appeals of his autocratic rulings were permitted. A decision by Landis was binding and permanent as if etched in stone, unless, of course, the commissioner changed his mind later.

Dickie Kerr of the White Sox, who was not involved in the 1919 scandal, tested the Reserve Clause in 1922 and was benched by Landis for three years. When Heinie Groh went to war with the Cincinnati Reds over his contract in 1921, Landis banned him for two days and then offered him a choice: Sign the deal or be banned for life. Groh signed.

Groh's teammate, Ray Fisher, balked at a $1,000 salary cut and asked for his outright release. Nothing doing, the Reds said. Fisher left for a college coaching job and was banned by Landis. The punishment lasted until 1980, when Bowie Kuhn reinstated him.

Pitcher Phil Douglas felt the Landis axe when he offered to disappear for a fee in the middle of a pennant race, and Philadelphia Phillies owner Bill Cox felt the commissioner's wrath when he was found to have bet on games. They were only sentimental bets, Cox said. No matter, said Landis. Cox was gone.

The commissioner was also a force in Washington and played an important role in the 1922 decision by Congress to exempt baseball from antitrust laws. He was a strident defender of the game's Reserve Clause, even though he believed the rule was patently illegal.

Landis was a conspicuous presence at the ballpark with his mane of white hair and his fierce look as he sat in the first row of seats, resting his arms on the low fence between the box seats and the field. It hardly disturbed fun-loving Chicago Cubs catcher Gabby Hartnett. One day during batting practice at Wrigley Field, Hartnett strolled over to the box seats to visit with underworld boss Al Capone. Landis was outraged and let Hartnett know it. The catcher's response was a classic: "If I visit his place of business," Hartnett said. "Why shouldn't he visit mine?"

Landis had strong opinions and never wavered from them. He adamantly opposed the integration of baseball, and it wasn't until after his death that Jackie Robinson became the first African-American player in modern baseball history. He also opposed the farm system innovation created by Branch Rickey, believing it would damage minor league baseball's owners. At various times, he declared whole groups of minor leaguers free from farm clubs, costing Major League teams considerable sums of money. Again, there was no appeal. Whatever Landis said was the way it would be.

There was one time when he did not apply aristocratic rule. When World War II began, he reached out to President Franklin D. Roosevelt, asking if Major League Baseball should shut down for the duration of the war. Roosevelt's response allowed baseball to continue. The correspondence became known as The Green Light letter.

Landis could trace his heritage to another war. His father, Dr. Abraham Landis, was a surgeon in the Union Army during the Civil War. The doctor was wounded at the battle of Kennesaw Mountain in northcentral Georgia during the war and decided to name his son after the encounter, accidentally spelling the name of the mountain with one "n" instead of two.

Landis was a high school dropout who passed through several jobs and employers before deciding to study the law. He received his law degree in 1891 and after finding himself on the federal bench, went on to change the course of baseball history.

CHAPTER 10

The Black Sox

If there was a pivotal year in the beginning of the 20th century, it was 1919. World War I had just ended and so had the pandemic flu outbreak that killed millions around the globe. Still ahead were the roaring twenties and the Jazz Age with its flappers and bathtub gin.

And then the Chicago White Sox fixed the World Series.

Baseball's landscape was littered with rumors and whispers about games that were rigged. Usually one or two players were involved in shenanigans. The White Sox, however, took it to a new level, when eight players were charged with throwing the World Series to the Cincinnati Reds.

The Series was just getting its footing as the crown jewel of the sports calendar, the culmination of a summer's worth of baseball. It had overcome the churlish behavior of Giants manager John McGraw, who caused it to be canceled in 1904 because of long-standing personal antagonisms. The Series was flourishing, so much so that it caught the attention of bigtime gamblers like Arnold Rothstein.

Rothstein was a gambler and racketeer. He ran a successful gambling casino and had horse racing interests at a time when races were often fixed. He also recognized Prohibition as a business opportunity to provide people with illicit alcohol. His interest in baseball was spurred by an eclectic community headlined by Abe Attell, the former featherweight champion of the world; Joseph (Sport) Sullivan, a Boston-based bettor and bookmaker; (Sleepy) Bill Burns, a former Major League pitcher and smalltime gambler; and Billy Maharg (Graham spelled backward), another ex-fighter and once a replacement player when the Detroit Tigers went on strike in 1912. They are said to have approached Rothstein with the scheme. Although Rothstein always denied being involved, it is hard to believe that a gambler with his reputation would not have been in this kind of major enterprise.

The White Sox offered a fertile opportunity. The owner of the team, Charles Comiskey, was almost universally disliked by his players for his penurious nature. He would not spend an extra dollar on the team if he could avoid it. There was the case of Eddie Cicotte, one of the best pitchers on the White Sox staff. His contract for 1919 carried a bonus clause for 30 victories. When Cicotte got to 29, Comiskey ordered him shut down. He would not get a chance for that 30th victory and the accompanying bonus.

The seeds for the fix were planted in a meeting between Cicotte, Sport Sullivan and first baseman Chick Gandil in a Boston hotel room. Cicotte and Gandil were part of a divided White Sox clubhouse. Catcher Ray Schalk, second baseman Eddie Collins and pitcher Dickie Kerr were in one group, which came to be known as the Clean Sox. Other players were open to offers from gamblers because of their dislike for Comiskey. Cicotte was an easy target because he had recently purchased a farm and was carrying a hefty mortgage. He had counted on the 30-win bonus. When he didn't get it, he was only too happy to talk with Gandil and Sport Sullivan.

At first, Gandil resisted. The World Series could not be fixed, he told Sullivan. To which Sullivan replied it could because it had been fixed before. He was probably referring to the 1918 Series between Boston and the Chicago Cubs, which was nearly halted by a player strike.

Slowly, the targeted players were recruited for the fix. Following Cicotte and Gandil were pitcher Lefty Williams, outfielder Joe Jackson, shortstop Swede Risberg, outfielder Happy Felsch, infielder Fred McMullin and third baseman Buck Weaver. The group included Chicago's two best pitchers (Cicotte and Williams) and best hitter (Jackson). A meeting at New York's Ansonia Hotel laid the foundation for the fix. The payoff would be $100,000 for the players. Weaver was at the meeting, but refused to participate in the fix. Nevertheless, he did not report it and was lumped in with the seven other conspirators.

Slowly the word spread through the gambling community that the White Sox would be doing business in this Series. The whispers were widespread. If the money could be raised in time, the Series would be fixed. It was a battle, but the day before the Series was to start, Cicotte found $10,000 on the pillow in his hotel room. Jackson found $5,000.

The gamblers needed a guarantee that the White Sox would, indeed, throw the World Series. It would come in the first inning of the first game, with Cicotte pitching for the White Sox. The signal would be Cicotte allowing Cincinnati leadoff batter Morrie Rath to reach base, either by walking him or hitting him. Cicotte's second pitch nailed Rath squarely in the back.

The fix was on.

Cicotte was pounded for seven hits and six runs in less than four innings as Cincinnati won the opener 9-1. After the game, Ray Schalk, the Chicago catcher, was seething. Cicotte had kept shaking him off, refusing to throw the pitches Schalk wanted. The catcher suspected something was up.

In Game 2, Lefty Williams walked three batters in the fourth inning and then gave up a triple to Larry Kopf in a 4-2 Cincinnati win. It was suspicious because Williams was a control specialist who had walked just 58 batters in 297 innings during the regular season. Again, Schalk's signals were ignored. He went to manager Kid Gleason, and soon Comiskey, National League president John Heydler and American League President Ban Johnson were told what was happening. They dismissed it.

After the White Sox won Game 3 3-0 on a three-hitter by rookie Dickie Kerr, who was not a part of the conspiracy, Cicotte returned for Game 4 and made two errors in the fifth inning, allowing both Cincinnati runs to score in a 2-0 Reds victory. With Williams back for Game 5, the

Reds scored four runs in the sixth inning, helped along by an error by Felsch, and won again, 5-0.

The gamblers were cashing in, but the White Sox were not. Angered by the slow payoffs, the Sox used Kerr in Game 6 and won 5-4 in 10 innings with Gandil's infield hit driving in the winning run. Jackson and Gandil had two hits apiece and each scored a run. Weaver, the clean conspirator, contributed three hits. Cicotte, after two subpar outings, looked more like himself in Game 7 in a complete game 4-1 victory.

The gamblers were not amused, and there were reports that some of the players' families would be targeted if the Black Sox did not cooperate. The word before Game 8 was that Cincinnati would gang up on Lefty Williams in the first inning, and that's exactly what happened. The Reds got five hits and four runs in the first inning, en route to a 10-5 victory that secured the Series, five games to three.

In the eight games, Gandil batted .231, Risberg hit .080 and committed four errors, Felsch hit .192 and had two errors. Weaver (.324) and Jackson (.375) hit well, and McMullin, a bench player, was a nonfactor with just two at-bats. Cicotte and Williams lost five games between them.

By August 1920, the buzz about a fixed World Series was widespread. That's when a game between the Philadelphia Phillies and Chicago Cubs came under some scrutiny. A grand jury was seated to investigate that game and baseball gambling in general, and that's when the Black Sox scandal began to unravel.

After gambler Billy Maharg testified that he had been in on Arnold Rothstein's plot to fix the 1919 World Series, Ed Cicotte and Shoeless Joe Jackson were called before the grand jury and implicated themselves. Cicotte said he needed the money because of family obligations. As he left the courthouse, Jackson was confronted by a youngster who said, "Say it ain't so, Joe."

The outfielder said nothing.

Soon Lefty Williams and Happy Felsch confessed their involvement. By October of 1920, the eight Chicago players were indicted, doomed to forever after be known as the Black Sox. The case went to trial in June 1921, but the prosecution's case collapsed when the confessions of the players mysteriously disappeared. There were suspicions that Charles Comiskey or Arnold Rothstein had arranged to have the documents stolen, dooming the state's case against the players. On Aug. 2, 1921, the eight players were found innocent of all charges.

Major League Baseball was rocked by the suspicions, the whispers, the strange play of the Chicago team and everything surrounding the World Series. Until then, the game had been presided over by a three-man commission. Now, however, the proprietors of the sport decided that system needed an overhaul. That's when they approached Judge Kenesaw Mountain Landis.

Landis was a stern federal judge, a no-nonsense arbiter, just the kind of man the owners thought could crack down on the suspicious activity that threatened the very fabric of their sport. In 1920, as the investigation of the World Series was heating up, he was offered the job of commissioner. He would act as a sort of court of last resort, with the three-man commission still in place. Landis refused. He would become commissioner, he said, but only if he were allowed to rule the game alone. With few options, the owners agreed to his demands. On Nov. 12, 1920, Kenesaw Mountain Landis became baseball's first czar, and it didn't take him long to demonstrate that he meant business.

Landis watched with interest the progress of the Black Sox trial. On the day after the eight players were found not guilty in court, the new commissioner issued his own definitive verdict.

"Regardless of the outcome of juries," he wrote, "no player that throws a ball game, no player that entertains proposals or promises to throw a game, no player that sits in conference with a bunch of crooked players where the ways and means of throwing games are discussed and does not promptly tell his club about it, will ever again play professional baseball."

The eight Black Sox players were done for life.

CHAPTER 11

The Conspirators

EDDIE CICOTTE

At a time when pitchers relied on a basic arsenal built around a fastball and spitball, Eddie Cicotte came up with something different. The slender right-hander was the first pitcher to master the knuckleball, a kind of trick pitch that behaved unpredictably. The knuckler was central to a barrage of pitches Cicotte used to baffle batters, and that made him one of the best pitchers of his era.

It also made him an attractive target when gamblers sought to fix the 1919 World Series.

Cicotte began his big league career with the Detroit Tigers and then spent five seasons with the Boston Red Sox, winning 62 games. But he was often at odds with club ownership before Boston sold him to the Chicago White Sox. By then, he had a full assortment of trick pitches to use against hitters — the shine ball, doctored with talcum powder, the scuffed-up emery ball, the spitball with a foreign substance applied to the ball and, of course, the knuckleball.

With the White Sox, he became one of the American League's best pitchers, leading the league with 28 wins and a 1.53 earned run average in 1917 and then again with 29 wins in 1919. He was a clubhouse prankster who liked to have fun with his teammates. But there was a serious side to him as well, and it had to do with money.

He was struggling financially, supporting a large family and making as little as White Sox owner Charles Comiskey could get away with paying him. So when the gamblers offered $10,000 for his cooperation in the 1919 World Series, Cicotte bought into the plot. He demanded the money in advance and found the cash on his pillow before he was to start the opening game of the Series against Cincinnati. When Cicotte hit leadoff batter Morrie Rath with his second pitch of the opener, it was a signal to gamblers that the fix was on.

After he was battered in a 9-1 loss in the opener, Cicotte returned in Game 4 and, despite his reputation as one of the best fielding pitchers in the game, made two crucial errors that led to a 2-0 loss. When gamblers were slow to pay off the players, the White Sox decided to reverse the tables and play to win. Cicotte's contribution to that effort was a 4-1 victory in Game 7 that more resembled his effective pitching. When the conspirators' families were threatened, the Black Sox cooperated in the next game, losing it 10-5 and the Series five games to three.

Despite the buzz about the Series being fixed, Cicotte

returned to the Sox and won 21 games in 1920. But when a grand jury was seated to examine gambling in baseball that year, Cicotte was called to testify and admitted that he had participated in fixing the 1919 World Series.

Cicotte and the other conspirators were found not guilty by the jury but not by Commissioner Kenesaw Mountain Landis, who threw all of them out of baseball. The knuckleball specialist won 208 games in his career but is better remembered for the two he lost in the 1919 World Series.

HAPPY FELSCH

The Black Sox scandal and Happy Felsch's participation as one of the players involved in the fix led to the end of what might have been a fine baseball career.

Purchased from the minor leagues by the White Sox in 1915, Felsch had 11 triples in his rookie season and 10 in each of the next two years. He batted .300 and .308 in the next two seasons and drove in 102 runs in 1917, second most in the American League and the first White Sox player to have more than 100 RBIs in a season. In the 1917 World Series against the New York Giants, he hit a home run in the opening game, helping roommate Eddie Cicotte to a 2-1 victory.

After missing the 1918 season while serving in World War I, Felsch returned to the Sox and batted .275 in 1919 and played a flawless center field. Blessed with a strong arm, he led the American League outfielders in putouts and assists, threw out 32 runners that season and was a solid performer.

And then came the fix.

Felsch, who had starred in the 1917 World Series when Chicago won the World Championship, was paid $5,000 for his participation in the fix, just about twice his salary from the White Sox that season. He had one of the poorest World Series of any of the conspirators with a .192 batting average and two crucial errors. It was an uncharacteristic performance by the center fielder, who had been one of the team's more dependable players.

Perhaps troubled by a guilty conscience, Felsch returned in 1920 and had one of the best seasons for any player in club history. He hit a career-high .338 with 14 home runs and 115 runs batted in. He had 69 extra base hits, 300 total bases and a .540 slugging percentage. It was all forgotten, however, when he found himself implicated in the fix and the trial that followed. When crucial evidence disappeared, all of the indicted players were found not guilty by the jury that heard the case. The next day, they were barred from baseball by Commissioner Kenesaw Mountain Landis.

At age 28, Happy Felsch's promising Major League career was over.

CHICK GANDIL

There was some history between Chicago White Sox first baseman Chick Gandil and team owner Charles Comiskey that may have played a part in the plan to fix the 1919 World Series.

Gandil had some bad experiences with authorities before he ever got to Chicago. He played for Shreveport in 1908, and when the St. Louis Browns wanted to return him there the next season, he signed instead with Fresno of the outlaw California State League. Threatened with being banned from organized baseball, Gandil thought better of that idea and went to Sacramento. He took with him $225 that did not belong to him, causing authorities to arrest him.

Once that unpleasantness was settled, Gandil moved on to Chicago in 1910, where he struggled, batting just .191. That led Comiskey to send him to minor league Montreal. Because the deal was made with less than 10 days remaining in the minor league season, Gandil demanded his full major league salary. He did not get it, and that decision left the first baseman angry and resentful. He would get even eventually.

After a solid 1911 season with Montreal, Gandil was traded to the Washington Senators, where he established major league credentials, batting .305 and leading the league in fielding percentage for the first of four times. He batted .318 the next year and seemed set with the Senators except for one small problem. He was a chain smoker who would light up between innings, annoying manager Clark Griffith. This led Washington to send Gandil to Cleveland for one year, where his average dipped to .259.

Traded back to his original White Sox team in 1917, Gandil became a fixture at first base as Chicago won the pennant and the World Series. But by then, the team was splitting into two factions — the Clean Sox, led by college-educated second baseman Eddie Collins, and the down and dirty group that despised owner Charles Comiskey, led by his old adversary, Chick Gandil.

Comiskey had cut expenses wherever he could after World War I ended, and one of the places he cut was Gandil's salary. The first baseman was furious, and it was not hard to convince him when he met with gambler Sport Sullivan to talk about fixing the World Series. He is said to have recruited his teammates in the scheme.

Just as Sport Sullivan had little trouble selling the World Series conspiracy to Gandil, the White Sox first baseman found recruiting others in the plot to be no problem. That's how deep the resentment toward Comiskey reached. Shortstop Swede Risberg signed on, along with pitchers Eddie Cicotte and Lefty Williams. The players enlisted slugger Joe Jackson, who probably didn't know what he was getting into, and center fielder Happy Felsch. Third baseman Buck Weaver knew about the plan but never agreed to participate. Reserve infielder Fred McMullin learned what was going on and asked to be included.

When Commissioner Kenesaw Mountain Landis banished the eight White Sox players, Gandil shrugged it off. He was 34 years old and ready to retire from the major leagues anyway. And unlike the other conspirators who got very little from the adventure, Gandil left with a hefty sum for orchestrating the fix of the 1919 World Series. He went on to play in other regional leagues, often with former Chicago teammates, who also had been banned by Landis. He always denied any involvement in the fix.

• • •

SHOELESS JOE JACKSON

Slugging outfielder Shoeless Joe Jackson blundered into the conspiracy orchestrated by others who were more sophisticated than he was. Jackson was illiterate and likely signed on to the fix out of loyalty to his teammates, but his raw ability made throwing the games a complicated matter.

Jackson was blessed with an abundance of pure baseball talent. His .357 career batting average, which includes a .408 rookie record season in 1911, is the third highest in history. He led the American League in triples three times and was an outstanding defensive player, equipped with a strong throwing arm. Shoeless Joe was the perfect player. But he also was illiterate. He never learned to read or write and was an easy foil for the conspirators, who included his name when negotiating with the gamblers to fix the Series.

Jackson came to the major leagues first with the Philadelphia Athletics. But the small town Southern native was overcome by a city of two million and ridden unmercifully by teammates who saw him as a hayseed to be harassed. He left the team twice, and finally Connie Mack traded him to Cleveland. It was with that team that Shoeless Joe became a star. But with the Federal League shopping for talent, there was the possibility that he might jump to the new league. That, coupled with Cleveland struggling with finances, pushed Jackson to the trading block, and he was swapped to the White Sox for $31,500 and three players. It was, at the time, baseball's most expensive transaction.

Jackson flourished with the White Sox, blossoming into one of baseball's biggest stars. That's what made him attractive to the gamblers seeking to fix the 1919 World Series.

Promised $20,000 for his participation in the plot, Jackson received $5,000 and tried to give it back. He also tried to talk with White Sox owner Charles Comiskey before the Series about the conspiracy but never was able to reach his boss. So Jackson did the one thing he could do best — play the games. He collected a record 12 hits, led all hitters with a .375 batting average with one home run and six runs batted in and did not commit an error in the eight games. If he was fixing the World Series, he was going about it in a very odd way.

When it was over, Jackson sought a meeting with Comiskey again but again failed to see his boss. Once again, he decided to do what he did best in 1920, and the result was a banner season. Shoeless Joe batted .382, drove in a career-best 121 runs and led the league with 20 triples.

But the conspiracy to fix the 1919 World Series was beginning to come apart. Summoned by a grand jury investigating gambling in baseball, Jackson confessed about his role in the fix. During the trial, a youngster approached Jackson outside the courtroom and pleaded, "Say it ain't so, Joe. Say it ain't so."

But it was so, and Jackson and seven of his teammates were banned from baseball because of their involvement in the fix, depriving one of the game's greatest players of a place in the Hall of Fame.

FRED MCMULLIN

Of all the players involved in the plot to fix the 1919 World Series, Fred McMullin was probably the unlikeliest participant.

A utility infielder who never played in more than 70 games in his five major league seasons, McMullin was not in any position to affect the outcome of the games. But because he hung out in the right places, he overheard conversations about the scheme between Chick Gandil and Swede Risberg, two of the main conspirators. McMullin threatened to tell management what was going on, and that's when he was invited to join the fix.

McMullin was a hotshot prospect when the Detroit Tigers purchased his contract from Tacoma in 1914. But the Tigers infield was crowded with stars, and McMullin had just one at-bat, striking out. Back in the minors with the Los Angeles Angels the next season, McMullin caught the attention of the White Sox, who purchased his contract. Once again, however, he was caught in a traffic jam of quality infielders. A broken leg cost him a month and when he returned to action, he was an extra hand on the White Sox roster.

But he became a hero one day in 1917 in Boston when a flock of fans charged on the field, demanding that a game being played in the rain be called. It was believed they were gamblers, trying to protect their bets. McMullin got involved in chasing them off the field. It was his first involvement with gamblers. It would not, however, be his last.

In the World Series that year, he was pressed into action in a shakeup of the Chicago lineup. But he hit just .125, including just one hit in his last 16 at-bats, and was a nonfactor as the White Sox defeated the New York Giants in six games.

Buck Weaver, Risberg and McMullin were in a rotation

on the left side of Chicago's infield for a while, but eventually McMullin settled into a backup role. That was his situation when he learned of the plot to fix the Series and asked to be included. In the 1919 World Series, McMullin batted just twice with one hit, the least involved of all the players who fixed the event. Nevertheless, he collected a $5,000 payoff, was indicted with the others and thrown out of baseball by Commissioner Kenesaw Mountain Landis in the aftermath of the trial.

The irony here is that after he left baseball, Fred McMullin, disgraced as one of the Black Sox conspirators, went into law enforcement, working for the Los Angeles office of the United States Marshal.

SWEDE RISBERG

The youngest participant in the Black Sox scandal was Swede Risberg, who, at the age of 25, found himself barred from baseball because of his involvement in the affair.

Risberg was a light hitting shortstop whose defensive ability kept him in the lineup. Frequently, manager Kid Gleason would become frustrated by Risberg's struggles at the plate and bench him. But sooner or later, it seemed, Risberg's glove would earn him a return to the starting lineup.

In 1919, Risberg batted a respectable .256 as the White Sox won the pennant and headed into the World Series, heavily favored against the Cincinnati Reds. When the plot to fix the outcome of the Series began to take shape, Risberg quickly became involved. Chick Gandil approached Risberg early in the plan, and the shortstop became one of the ringleaders, recruiting teammates for the fix and arranging for payoffs as a middle man between the gamblers and the players.

Occasionally, there were threats that the plot might disintegrate. Shoeless Joe Jackson, for one, was never an enthusiastic participant, and when he began to consider bailing out, Risberg confronted him and threatened his life. The shortstop had become the enforcer for the fix.

On the field, Risberg played his role to the hilt. He batted .080 with two hits in 25 at-bats and made four errors, including a crucial one in the opening game when he failed to complete a critical double play, helping the Reds score five runs against Chicago ace Eddie Cicotte, another one of the conspirators.

The next season, with rumors swirling about the fixed World Series, Risberg responded with his finest season, batting .266 with 21 doubles, 10 triples and 65 runs batted in. In the final month, with a grand jury beginning to investigate gambling in baseball, Risberg went on a tear, batting .380 in his final 13 games. Shortly after that, Eddie Cicotte appeared before the grand jury and confessed.

Risberg was not good at keeping secrets. At the beginning of the plot, he called an old pal, St. Louis Browns infielder Joe Gedeon, and told him that he might want to bet on the Reds in the Series because the White Sox were doing business with gamblers. When Chicago owner Charles Comiskey later offered a $20,000 bounty for information on the fix, Gedeon stepped forward. He did not get the payoff and instead wound up being banned from baseball, just like Risberg and the rest of the Black Sox.

BUCK WEAVER

The conspiracy to fix the 1919 World Series was constructed in a couple of player meetings organized by Chick Gandil and Swede Risberg. Buck Weaver was at both meetings but wanted no part of the fix. Weaver insisted he would play the World Series straight.

Weaver was an important cog in Chicago's lineup. He was a slick fielding switch hitter who batted .296 with a career-high 45 extra base hits in the White Sox's championship season. That made him an excellent target for the fixers. But he was having none of it. He turned his back on the conspiracy. So the Black Sox went about their business with no help from Weaver and deliberately lost the World Series, despite being heavily favored. The 1919 World Series was played with a black cloud over it.

Weaver's honesty did him no good. He was banned from baseball for life along with the other Black Sox because he had not reported what he knew about the plot. It seemed harsh treatment for the man who hit .324 in the Series, with four doubles, a triple and four runs scored, and played errorless ball at third base.

The next year, Weaver went on a tear, enjoying his best season with a .331 batting average, 208 hits and a .365 on-base percentage. But the buzz about fixed games was growing louder than ever, and the Black Sox scandal came apart when one of the gamblers, Bill Maharg, talked publicly about it. The next day, White Sox owner Charles Comiskey had letters of suspension delivered to the players involved. And Buck Weaver was included.

Because Weaver played no role in fixing the games, he

generated plenty of sympathy. Even the judge who presided over the trial noted that the third baseman was a victim of circumstances. It made no difference. Commissioner Kenesaw Mountain Landis was giving no quarter in the wake of the scandal. In his statement announcing the bans, Landis was direct, stating, "No player that sits in a conference where the ways and means of throwing games are planned and discussed and does not promptly tell his club about it, will ever play professional baseball."

It was as if the statement was aimed directly at Weaver, who was swept away with the rest of the Black Sox. At age 29, Buck Weaver was banished from baseball.

Weaver frequently pleaded for leniency. A petition with 14,000 signatures asked for his reinstatement. Commissioner Landis shrugged off his pleas, instead releasing a statement that said, "Birds of a feather flock together. Men associating with gamblers and crooks could expect no leniency." Landis' successors, Happy Chandler and Ford Frick, also stood fast on the ban.

In the years after the Black Sox trial and Landis' edict, Weaver continued to play ball on the semipro circuit and sometimes in outlaw leagues. His teammates were often players swept out of the game by Landis, including his old Black Sox teammates Happy Felsch, Lefty Williams, Swede Risberg and Chick Gandil.

LEFTY WILLIAMS

When he took the mound for the final game of the 1919 World Series, Lefty Williams of the Chicago White Sox was a nervous wreck.

The curveball control artist had signed on with a half dozen teammates, conspiring to fix the Series and allow underdog Cincinnati to win. His payoff was to be $10,000, a nice piece of cash for a player earning just $500 a month. But the gamblers had been slow to pay up, leading the players to decide on a change in the program. They would try to win instead of lose.

When more cash trickled in, the fix was back on. And by the way, if Lefty Williams didn't cooperate as planned, his life and his family would be in danger.

Williams, a 23-game winner in the regular season, had already played his part in the fix in his first two starts in the Series. He was unusually wild in Game 2, walking six batters in a 4-2 loss. This from a pitcher who walked just 56 batters in nearly 300 innings during the regular season. Catcher Ray Schalk was livid and confronted Williams in the clubhouse before teammates separated them.

The promised payoff came after Game 4, with $5,000 for Williams and $5,000 for Shoeless Joe Jackson. Comforted by the arrival of the cash, Williams had another bad outing in Game 5, allowing four runs in the sixth inning in a rally fueled by a double by opposing pitcher Hod Eller.

By the time Game 8 arrived, the Black Sox were restless again because of the slow payoffs. The rumor was they might play to win. There was no chance that Williams would be part of the reversal, however, after he was threatened by the mob behind the fix. He was shelled in the first inning, knocked out after facing just five batters and retiring only one. The Reds scored four runs before Chicago ever came to bat en route to a 10-5 victory that clinched the Series.

Williams' pitching line for three World Series starts

— all losses — was 12 hits, 12 runs and eight walks in 16 1/3 innings. He came back to win 22 games in 1920 before the trial and Commissioner Kenesaw Mountain Landis' decision to ban him and the seven other Black Sox from baseball.

CHAPTER 12

The Eight Black Sox Plus One

Joe Gedeon was an innocent bystander to the 1919 Black Sox scandal. A fine fielding second baseman, he spent seven years in the major leagues with the Washington Senators, the New York Yankees and St. Louis Browns and was once part of a blockbuster trade that included Hall of Famer Eddie Plank. He never played for the Chicago White Sox, but he had friends on that troubled team and ultimately, that's what did him in.

Gedeon was a West Coast guy who grew up in California. So he was not exactly thrilled when he was drafted by the Philadelphia Athletics in 1912 and passed along to the Washington Senators. He was spooked by an East Coast blizzard when he arrived for training camp in 1913 and refused to report until a week or so later when the snow had cleared.

He had some solid minor league seasons, including

1915, when he hit .317, had a record 67 doubles and stole 25 bases for Salt Lake City in an extended Pacific Coast League schedule. He hoped to jump to the Federal League the next season, but when that league folded, he wound up with the Yankees. After two unimpressive seasons in New York, he was shipped to St. Louis, where he made the acquaintance of some nefarious characters.

Gambling was rampant in baseball in those days, and Gedeon participated in that pastime with his new friends. One of his old pals was Swede Risberg, the White Sox shortstop and a central figure in the fixed World Series. And Risberg was something of a blabbermouth. When the conspiracy to throw the World Series was in place, Risberg called some friends and urged them to bet on Cincinnati. One of those friends was Joe Gedeon, who had a knack for hanging out with shady characters. He had contacts in the St. Louis betting community and was friendly with another California ballplayer, the notorious Hal Chase.

Gedeon knew Risberg from their days together in the Pacific Coast League, where he also played with White Sox pitcher Lefty Williams and infielder Fred McMullin. He was a teammate of Chick Gandil in Washington. These were his pals, and they were all in on the World Series conspiracy. It didn't take long for Risberg to clue Gedeon in, and the infielder made some wagers.

After the Series ended, with rumors of the fix resonating everywhere, White Sox owner Charles Comiskey offered a $10,000 reward for information on the conspiracy. Gedeon was happy to oblige at that price. The two men talked, but Comiskey decided Gedeon's information was useless, certainly not worth the $10,000 reward. The infielder left the owner's office with no payoff for his trouble.

The next season, with chatter about the fix reaching a cacophony and a grand jury in place to investigate betting in baseball, Gedeon was terrified. He had been having a good season with the Browns, but in the final weeks, he lost 20 pounds and his batting average dipped below .300. The heat was on, and Gedeon was feeling it.

Eddie Cicotte, Joe Jackson and Lefty Williams all appeared before the grand jury and confessed. They were suspended immediately, a major impact on the 1920 pennant race, which was won by Cleveland. Eventually, Gedeon was called to testify and held nothing back. Yes, he knew about the fix. Yes, he bet on the games. Yes, he won some money, but not exactly a windfall.

When the verdict was delivered, eight White Sox players were found innocent and walked away from the charges, although not from the cloud that hung over them. Commissioner Kenesaw Mountain Landis was less lenient, immediately banning the eight players. And, oh yes, Joe Gedeon was thrown out of baseball as well. That's because he knew what was going on all the time, and in Landis' mind, that made him as guilty as the players who had fixed the games.

Gedeon was one more victim of baseball's worst gambling scandal and the only one who was not a member of the Black Sox team. There would be more scandals and more victims. Rarely, however, were they more peripheral in the affair than Joe Gedeon.

CHAPTER 13

One That Got Away

In the days and months after the 1919 Black Sox scandal, baseball resolved to clean up the game and hired federal judge Kenesaw Mountain Landis to do that job. Landis brought with him a king-sized broom to sweep away anyone who was even on the periphery of the fixed World Series.

Rube Benton, who by his own admission certainly qualified, was not one of them.

Benton was a talented left-handed pitcher who lived life on the edge, enjoying gambling, alcohol and carousing, activities which occasionally interfered with his baseball career. He had effective stretches like 1914, when he won 16 games and threw four shutouts for the last place Reds. Of course, a good behavior clause in his contract may have had something to do with that. But he sometimes went missing in action, a habit that annoyed his employers. In 1915, the Cincinnati Reds ran out of patience and placed him on waivers. And that's when Benton's career began taking an odd turn.

New York Giants manager John McGraw delighted in his ability to rehabilitate lost individuals and put in a waiver claim for $3,000. Behaving like the waiver process was some kind of game of high-stakes poker, the Pittsburgh Pirates raised McGraw, offering $4,000. The extra $1,000 carried the day, and while McGraw filed a protest, Benton reported to the Pirates and was immediately pressed into action, pitching a six-hitter to defeat the Chicago Cubs. It was a brief stopover for him. The National League upheld the Giants protest and sent Benton to New York, where his first start came against his old pals from Pittsburgh, who beat him handily.

But what of his start for the Pirates against the Cubs? That game was scrubbed from the record books. It was if it had never happened.

When he was available, Benton was reasonably effective for the Giants. He won 16 games in 1916 and 15 more the next season, when he pitched the first shutout by a left-hander in World Series history against the Chicago White Sox. But he failed to cover home plate on a game-turning rundown play that left Heinie Zimmerman chasing Eddie Collins across the plate with the winning run in the deciding game of the Series. And more trouble was on the horizon for baseball and Benton.

Gambling and fixes were widespread during that period, but nobody had attempted to mess with the World Series until 1919, when the White Sox succumbed to a scheme to throw the Series to the Cincinnati Reds. When the rumors of the fix became widespread, a grand jury was convened, and one of the witnesses was Rube Benton. His testimony was so riveting that he was called before the grand jury twice.

Why of course, Benton said, he was aware of the fix. He had been in a New York hotel room when one of the fixers, "Sleepy Bill" Burns, called to advise a Giants teammate that the fix was on. He heard that Hal Chase won $40,000, and a friendly bookmaker in Cincinnati had revealed to him the names of the eight White Sox players who were involved. But the report that Benton himself had won $3,800 betting on the Series, well, that was just not true, a rumor spread by ex-teammate Buck Herzog after Benton told the grand jury that he had been approached by Chase and Herzog to fix another game. Of course, the rumor was supported by a couple of affidavits from Boston teammates Tony Boeckel and Art Wilson.

Benton was the star witness in the hearing and seemed none the worse for the experience at the start of the next season when he pitched well for the Giants, winning five games. Then, quite suddenly, he was gone, released and unable to find any other club willing to sign him. He was termed "undesirable." It was like a black cloud (or was it a blacklist?) had suddenly settled over the left-hander.

Benton surfaced in 1922 with St. Paul of the American Association and flourished there, winning 24 games. That caught the attention of the Cincinnati Reds and St. Louis Browns, who thought he could help them. But almost as soon as they expressed interest, they were advised to back off by National League president John Heydler and American League president Ban Johnson. Benton would not be welcomed back in either league. Inevitably, the matter landed on the desk of Commissioner Landis, who had been barring just about any player found to have been anywhere near the Black Sox scandal. Even vague knowledge of what was going on was enough to get Joe Gedeon bounced from baseball. Gedeon had testified to the grand jury, admitted he was pals with some of the fixers and had won a couple of hundred dollars betting on the Series. Landis banned him for life. Surely Benton would join him.

But he didn't.

In a burst of goodwill, the commissioner ruled that Benton could return to baseball's good graces. He had pitched without incident in the minors. He could pitch again in the majors. Everyone else who had the slightest involvement in the Black Sox Series was barred from baseball. Benton, however, was not. He returned to the Cincinnati Reds, where he pitched for three more seasons, winning 30 games. Then it was back to the American Association, where he pitched until he was 44 years old.

He finished his major league career with 150 wins. And that doesn't include the one game he won that didn't count for the Pittsburgh Pirates in 1915.

CHAPTER 14

Dickie Kerr's Ups and Downs

In baseball's darkest moment, Dickie Kerr was like a beam of sunshine, winning two games in the 1919 World Series while all around him, his teammates were trying to lose them.

After the Chicago Black Sox lost the first two games in the best-of-nine series to the Cincinnati Reds, Kerr responded with a brilliant three-hit shutout, one of the best pitched games in World Series history. Then, when the fixers lost Game 4 and Game 5, Kerr came back to win Game 6.

He emerged from the Series as a hero, a clean player who overcame the shenanigans of eight teammates who either knew of or participated in the fix.

And then Dickie Kerr got banned from baseball.

Kerr was a pint-sized left-hander, just 5 foot 7 and 155 pounds and considered the fourth pitcher in the Chicago rotation behind Eddie Cicotte, Lefty Williams and Red Faber. As a rookie in 1919, he went 13-8 on a team that was divided into two factions. One group, angry with the penny-pinching policies of owner Charles Comiskey, conspired to fix the World Series. The other group, loyal to the franchise, played it straight.

Kerr was not in a position to influence either faction. He was, after all, just a rookie, a rotation afterthought, whose size was ridiculed. But when manager Kid Gleason discovered the fix, he turned to Kerr to bail out the team. The rookie had been used as both a reliever and starter but was hardly in the class of Cicotte and Williams. Still, Gleason gave him the ball for Game 3, leaving Cicotte, the probable starter, a bit flabbergasted.

Coming off the Game 3 shutout, and after Cicotte and Williams, two of the fixers, dropped the next two games, Kerr was the obvious choice to start Game 6, and he won again. The Series went eight games with Cincinnati winning baseball's only tainted championship.

Years later, Kerr said he knew what was going on with the Black Sox when fielders were a step slow getting to the ball or made bad throws or errors on balls that should have been caught. The bad feelings between teammates erupted during a game against Boston the next season, when a ball fell between Joe Jackson and Happy Felsch and then Buck Weaver and Swede Risberg made errors, costing Kerr runs. The pitcher confronted Weaver and Risberg on the bench. Catcher Ray Schalk, another of the Clean Sox, joined in, and there was nearly a riot before Kid Gleason separated the combatants.

Tempers were short because of the continuing questions about the 1919 World Series, which led to a grand jury investigation and the ensuing trial, which resulted in the bans of eight Black Sox players.

Kerr had established himself in that World Series and went 21-9 in 1920. He got into a squabble with Comiskey that year before agreeing to a rather skimpy contract. The next season, the White Sox roster was depleted by the loss of the eight players who were banned by Commissioner Kenesaw Mountain Landis. The Sox fell to seventh place, with Kerr going 19-17 and pitching a shutout in his final start of the season on a day when he was honored by the team.

It would be his last major league victory.

When he asked for a $500 raise the next year, Comiskey refused and the little left-hander went home. Baseball's Reserve Clause bound players to their teams and prohibited them from playing elsewhere. When Kerr showed up pitching for an independent team in a game against a team with players from the Black Sox, Landis acted swiftly. Dickie Kerr was banned, just like the players who threw the 1919 World Series.

Kerr spent the next three years pitching in outlaw leagues, away from organized baseball. It was as if he was pitching on a vaudeville circuit with stops in minor league outposts far removed from the majors. He was making a pretty good living but longed to return to Chicago. When he backed off the semipro leagues, Landis viewed it as retribution, and in August 1925, Kerr was reinstated. But at age 31, he was no longer the pitcher he had once been. He pitched in 12 games, lost his only decision and finished with a bloated 5.15 earned run average.

His pitching career was over, but his baseball career was not. Years later, he would have a major impact on the sport.

Kerr bounced around the low minor leagues as a manager for several years and, in 1940, found himself with the Daytona Beach Islanders of the Florida State League, a St. Louis Cardinals affiliate. One of the team's top prospects was a left-handed pitcher who had struggled with his control. This was the perfect pupil for Kerr, a left-hander who was a control specialist. Under his coaching, the young pitcher prospered, going 18-5 with a 2.62 earned run average.

With just a 14-man roster, players often did double duty, and the pitcher, who was also a pretty good hitter, saw time in the outfield. One day, he tried to make a diving catch. His spikes got caught in the turf, and he tumbled to the ground, landing hard on his left shoulder. The youngster came out of the fall with a sore shoulder that never quite healed. He thought the injury would end his baseball dreams. It did not. A promising pitching career was over. A dominant hitting career was just starting.

Kerr encouraged Stan Musial to stay with the game. His bat would be a ticket to the big leagues, the old pitcher promised. Kerr became a mentor, taking Musial and his wife into his home and driving Mrs. Musial to the hospital to deliver their first child.

The advice paid off. Musial went on to win seven batting titles and three Most Valuable Player Awards. He led the Cardinals into four World Series, and he never forgot the kindness Dickie Kerr once showed him. Years later, Musial bought a house for Kerr and paid tribute to his old manager, the man who saved a Hall of Fame career.

CHAPTER 15

You're Gone, Too

In the aftermath of the 1919 Black Sox World Series, Commissioner Kenesaw Mountain Landis applied a broad brush in expelling players from the game. Some did not deserve such harsh treatment. Ray Fisher was the perfect example.

A graduate of Middlebury College, Fisher pitched for the New York Highlanders, who later became the Yankees, from 1910–17 and was one of the best starters on a second division team. He won 73 games over eight seasons and was considered one of the better pitchers of the era. That was reflected in his salary of $6,500, a hefty paycheck for the time. After battling pleurisy related to tuberculosis through 1916 and 1917, Fisher missed the 1918 season, when he was drafted into the army.

When he returned for 1919, his contract had been sold to Cincinnati, and Reds management cut his salary to $3,500. Fisher was furious but had no alternative. He had been away from the game for a year and could not tell what effect that would have on his pitching. In fact, however, he enjoyed a fine comeback season, posting a 14-5 record with a 2.17 earned run average as the Reds won the National League pennant for the first time and advanced to the crooked World Series against the Black Sox.

Fisher started Game 3 of the Series and was beaten 3-0 on a three-hitter by Dickie Kerr, who was not involved in the fix. Chick Gandil, believed to be the architect of the Black Sox conspiracy, delivered a two-run double that scored Shoeless Joe Jackson and Happy Felsch, who were also implicated in the fix. Fisher's reward for his productive season was a raise — a $150 raise. It was about that time that Fisher began thinking about changing careers.

He had dabbled in college coaching while at Middlebury and thought that might be an alternative for him. Disgusted by his contract, Fisher expressed his displeasure to manager Pat Moran. Soon word reached Garry Herrmann, president of the team, who summoned Fisher to his office. The men talked briefly, and the pitcher emerged with a $1,500 raise. Still, the affair had left a bad taste in his mouth, and he decided to keep his options open. One of those options was to talk with Branch Rickey, who was managing St. Louis at the time but had contacts in the world of collegiate sports.

The pitcher had planted a seed. A year later, it bloomed when the Reds contract offer included a $1,000 cut. Fisher was furious, and he let Herrmann know it. He signed but was more determined than ever to find a job coaching college baseball. Meanwhile, Rickey had mentioned the pitcher to Michigan officials, and when coach Del Pratt left the school to return to Major League Baseball, Michigan contacted Fisher.

The pitcher left the Reds with his manager's permission to look over the Michigan opportunity. When he returned to the Reds, his mind was pretty much made up. He would retire from baseball and take the college job. Herrmann was frantic to keep the pitcher, offering to restore the $1,000 salary cut. Fisher demanded a three-year contract, which was out of the question for a 33-year-old pitcher as far as the Reds were concerned. Then, in a dramatic move worthy of a Hollywood moment, Fisher picked up the phone on Herrmann's desk and called Michigan to advise the school that he would take the coaching job.

Fisher asked to be released from his contract, and at first, Herrmann agreed to place the pitcher on the voluntarily retired list. A day later, however, Reds management changed that to the ineligible list. Herrmann was angered over reports that Fisher might surface with St. Louis after the college season ended. In a fit of pique, the Cincinnati boss argued that Fisher had given the Reds only seven days notice regarding his intention to leave instead of the 10 days required in player contracts. The matter went to National League president John Heydler and then landed on Landis' desk. After a brief investigation, the commissioner advised Fisher that he was banned from baseball for life because he had broken his contract.

It turned out, however, that the ban had some holes in it. Years later, Fisher received a lifetime pass to games from Major League Baseball, an act he interpreted to mean he was back in the game's good graces. He later worked as a spring training instructor for the Detroit Tigers and

Milwaukee Braves. Certainly someone banned from baseball for life could not do that.

Researchers later discovered that the ban had never been rescinded. The pitcher who had fought a $1,000 salary cut was still on the outside looking in. When Gerald Ford, by then president of the United States, led a legion of letter writers supporting the old coach, commissioner Bowie Kuhn decided to change Fisher's status in 1980, reinstating him as "a retired player in good standing."

It took 60 years, but Ray Fisher was no longer banned from baseball.

CHAPTER 16

Don't Get Too Cozy with Cozy

It was supposed to be a joke, a prank played by a crusty old coach on a part-time player for a good laugh. That's what Cozy Dolan said. But Kenesaw Mountain Landis didn't think it was funny, and that's how come Dolan and outfielder Jimmy O'Connell of the New York Giants were barred from baseball in 1924.

The Giants and Brooklyn Robins (later the Dodgers) were engaged in a tight pennant race as the season came down to the final weekend that season. Both were playing tail-end clubs, the Giants against Philadelphia, the Robins against Boston. New York was leading the race by 1 ½ games and needed just one more win to lock up a fourth straight pennant. Surely, they could manage that against a Phillies team buried in seventh place, 37 games behind, with nothing on the line. But strange things happen sometimes in baseball. Why not make sure?

So before the game on Sept. 27, Cozy Dolan approached Jimmy O'Connell with a suggestion. How about O'Connell approaching an old friend, Phillies shortstop Heinie Sand, with an offer? How about, say $500, to let up and help the Giants win?

Would Dolan really do that? The new commissioner had been on a tear cleaning up the game following the Black Sox World Series scandal of 1919. People were getting thrown out of baseball for the least impropriety. This would be a flat-out offer to fix a game. Would Dolan take that chance?

Of course not, the coach said. He was just kidding around.

And why would O'Connell be the messenger boy? He was a peripheral player on the Giants, limited to just 52 games as a reserve, hardly in a position to offer that kind of money to an opponent. Why would O'Connell be the choice to carry such an offer?

That's what Landis wanted to know, too.

Interestingly, Dolan and O'Connell had similar careers. Only twice in seven major league seasons had he played in more than 100 games. He was an extra hand outfielder, just like O'Connell. He came up with Cincinnati in 1909 and spent time with Pittsburgh, Philadelphia, St. Louis, the New York Highlanders and finally the Giants, where he became an aide to manager John McGraw. He was also baseball's second Cozy Dolan. The original played from 1885 to 1906.

Sand was shaken by the conversation with O'Connell. The two were pals, once roommates who grew up in the San Francisco area and played against each other in the Pacific

Coast League. The shortstop digested what O'Connell said, hesitated for a while because this was an old friend and then reported it to the Phillies manager, Art Fletcher. Within days, the matter was on the desk of the commissioner, who had taken a hard line with such matters since being hired in 1920.

Here was O'Connell, an educated man with a degree from Santa Clara University, a fringe player and probably an outsider in the raucous Giants clubhouse, easy pickings for a gag. And, apparently, Dolan had fellow conspirators in George Kelly, Frankie Frisch and Ross Youngs, all veterans, all interested in getting a good laugh. According to O'Connell, they also talked to him about approaching Sand. That said, O'Connell told the commissioner that Dolan was the main actor in the scheme, the one who sealed the deal. And yes, he had offered $500 to Sand.

The Giants won the game on Sept. 27 5-1, and when Brooklyn lost to Boston 3-2 that day, it clinched the pennant for New York. It did not, however, put a close to this messy matter of Dolan and O'Connell.

Landis held three days of hearings with the various participants. At first, Dolan said he couldn't remember any such thing happening. Later, he said he had not made the bribe suggestion to O'Connell. The commissioner was suspicious when the coach kept changing his story. The solution was to ban him from the game. And Landis had no choice when O'Connell confessed to offering the bribe to Sand. The commissioner threw him out, too.

As for the other three Giants, they all denied speaking to O'Connell about the plot. Landis bought their stories and let them off. There was some speculation that McGraw, the Giants manager, might have had a hand in the matter. After all, he had been down this road before when the Giants team doctor tried to bribe umpire Bill Klem before the Giants-Cubs playoff game in 1908. McGraw's name never came up in the O'Connell-Dolan affair, though, and he never managed a team to a pennant again.

Heinie Sand played four more undistinguished seasons with the Phillies. Dolan drifted into obscurity, insisting the whole story of the O'Connell-Sand affair would never be told. O'Connell wound up playing in the outlaw Copper/ Frontier League. There he played with other familiar names. Some of his teammates were outcasts like Hal Chase and Chick Gandil and others who had been run off from Major League Baseball by Kenesaw Mountain Landis.

CHAPTER 17

Shufflin' Along

Equipped with a strong right arm and a stronger thirst for adult beverages, Phil Douglas was a baseball puzzle. When he was sober, he mowed down enemy batters with an explosive fastball and one of baseball's best spitballs. The trouble was, he wasn't always sober. He had a habit of wandering off, sometimes for a day or two, sometimes for a week on what he termed "vacations." That made his availability to pitch questionable from day to day.

Trouble seemed to find Douglas, who was more accustomed to the laid-back rural lifestyle of his Southern upbringing than he was to the demands of organized baseball. In his rookie season with Cincinnati, he was fined $100 for violating training rules. It was the first of numerous fines imposed by teams on the big pitcher. A year later, he was suspended three times for drinking, wore out his welcome with the Reds and was sent packing to Brooklyn, where he was suspended again for breaking training rules, a polite way of saying he was drinking too much.

His next stop was Chicago, where his reputation preceded him. Sooner or later, managers and teams would run out of patience with the big right-hander, whose nickname was "Shufflin'," because of the easy gait he used getting to the mound. He was still in spring training in 1916 when manager Joe Tinker smelled alcohol on his breath and suspended him. Douglas claimed what Tinker smelled was garlic from a Spanish restaurant where the pitcher had eaten dinner. Tinker was having none of that, and the suspension stuck.

Tinker was gone in 1918, but Douglas was still a handful for new manager Fred Mitchell. The breaking point came during the World Series against Boston. Mitchell called on him in a crucial spot in Game 4. When Douglas threw away a sacrifice bunt, allowing the winning run to score, it sealed the pitcher's fate with the Cubs. Mitchell demanded that he be traded, explaining that he never knew where Douglas was or whether he was in shape to pitch.

So the Cubs dealt the pitcher to New York, where manager John McGraw believed he could rehabilitate even the most lost soul. Douglas, however, would be a major project for the Giants' manager. Nothing changed, though. Douglas took off for a "vacation" in his first season, incurring McGraw's wrath. Later, he showed up pitching semipro ball, which he preferred to McGraw's stern hand. This, the manager decided, was not going to be easy.

Eventually, Douglas made his way back to the Giants, ready to face more of McGraw's public bluster. One of the manager's tactics was to scream at offending players in front of the rest of the team. And just when it seemed that he had turned Douglas into a useful piece of his pitching staff, it all fell apart. Douglas won 15 games for the Giants in 1921 and two more in the World Series when he struck out Babe Ruth four times. Before the end of the next season, he was banned from baseball.

Douglas had an 11-4 record and 2.63 earned run average midway through 1922. He decided it was time for a break. When the pitcher failed to appear at the ballpark one day, McGraw exploded. Douglas never handled the manager's abuse very well and left determined to drown his anger with some liquid refreshment. He slipped away from coach Jesse Burkett, who was to serve as a bird dog watching over the pitcher, and when next located, he was sleeping off too many drinks in a friend's apartment. McGraw sent operatives to transport Douglas, first to a police station and then to a rehabilitation clinic, where he was sedated and treated with drugs for five days. When his treatment was done, the Giants sent the $500 bill for his stay to the pitcher, who was in no shape to pay it at that particular time.

After five more days away, Douglas surfaced at the Polo Grounds, staggering from his drug treatment and hardly fit to pitch. McGraw went into another one of his patented rages, dressing down Douglas in front of the team. The manager fined Douglas $100, enough to buy plenty of wine and beer and probably some cocktails as well, and suspended him without pay. Douglas was furious at the punishment and decided to get even. He chose a foolish method, however, and it cost him the rest of his career.

Douglas decided to send a letter to St. Louis outfielder Les Mann, an ex-teammate when both men played for the

Cubs. With the Cardinals and Giants engaged in a tight pennant race, the pitcher offered his friend a proposition. Pay him off and he would disappear, essentially robbing the Giants of one of their key pitchers in the middle of the pennant race and giving the Cardinals a major advantage.

"I want to leave here," Douglas wrote, "but I want some inducement. I don't want to see this guy (McGraw) win the pennant. You know I can pitch, and I am afraid if I stay, I will win the pennant for them. Talk this over with the boys and if it is all right, send the goods to my house at night, and I will go to the fishing camp. Let me know if you all want me to do this, and I will go home on the next train."

The pitcher picked the wrong customer. Mann was a straight shooter, who would not get involved in any shenanigans, especially with baseball still wounded from the Black Sox scandal. The outfielder went to the Cardinals front office with the letter, and it soon found its way to the desk of Kenesaw Mountain Landis. Predictably, the commissioner was not amused.

Meanwhile, Douglas realized his mistake and tried to contact Mann to destroy the letter. It was too late. Landis was on his way to a meeting with the pitcher and McGraw, and he had some bad news. Douglas was to be banned for life for his proposal. McGraw, in a burst of compassion, pleaded to give the pitcher a second chance. In Judge Landis' court, however, there were no second chances. Douglas was done, gone from baseball because of his fondness for liquor and a letter he never should have written.

CHAPTER 18

Leo the Lip

Leo Durocher was a scandal waiting to happen. Everywhere he went, trouble seemed to follow him. As a player, he once was accused of stealing Babe Ruth's wristwatch. As a manager, he was thrown out of 94 games for misbehaving with umpires. And as a bon vivant and man about town, he spent the off-seasons living in actor George Raft's house. It all caught up with Durocher in 1947, when Commissioner Happy Chandler suspended the man they called Leo the Lip for the entire season.

Chandler's explanation was that Durocher was running around with a fast crowd of Hollywood hustlers, gamblers and other disreputable characters. It didn't help that Durocher's old pal, Raft, played gangsters in the movies. Raft even paid a visit to the commissioner's office to clear the air. All of this reflected badly on baseball as did

Durocher's annoying habit of marrying and then divorcing a parade of beautiful women.

Durocher met Hollywood star Laraine Day in 1945. She happened to be married at the time, but this hardly interfered with his pursuit of the actress. In January 1947, rather than wait for her California divorce to become final, Day divorced her husband in Mexico and became Durocher's third of four wives the next day in El Paso, Texas. Her previous marriage was a small detail overlooked. This caused some serious conversation in baseball's executive suite because Leo the Lip was doing his Hollywood thing again.

Meanwhile, Durocher was a handful on the field, battling umpires endlessly, kicking dirt on them, calling them names and generally behaving badly. This resulted in a stream of ejections and numerous suspensions that was becoming disruptive for the Dodgers and for baseball. One of the classic confrontations came with the combative manager facing off with jumbo-sized umpire George Magerkurth. At the height of the argument, the much larger Magerkurth looked down at Durocher and said, "I'm going to reach down and bite your head off." Durocher replied, "If you do, you'll have more brains in your stomach than you do in your head."

Predictably, Durocher got the thumb.

In another argument, while kicking dirt in a style that Earl Weaver or Billy Martin would admire, Durocher's spike caught the shin of umpire Jocko Conlan. The manager was thrown out that time, too.

There were occasional fistfights, sometimes with fans who heckled him, sometimes with reporters who questioned him. Durocher did not accept criticism warmly. He teased opponents, defending the edge he brought to the ballpark but reminding listeners that it didn't pay to be nice. One day, talking about Mel Ott, he observed what a nice guy the Giants manager was and, although he never said it in exactly those words, the message was clear that nice guys finish last.

And, of course, there was always the matter of gambling, card playing and his association with some shady characters. Durocher enjoyed assorted games of chance, once even ordering champagne for the house after winning a large pot of cash at a bingo party. Bingo, however, was tame stuff for Durocher, who could play poker or roll dice at a moment's notice. Chandler warned him to cut it out. Durocher's response was to call the commissioner's attention to a couple of gamblers sitting in a field box with Yankees owner Larry MacPhail. It was MacPhail who had hired Durocher to manage the Dodgers in 1941, touching off a long-standing feud between two strong-willed and short-tempered individuals. The eccentric MacPhail would routinely fire the loudmouth Durocher for a misdemeanor real or imagined and then hire him back the next day, sometimes the next hour.

When MacPhail left the Dodgers to join the New York Yankees, it created a dandy cross-town feud that increased in intensity when the Yankees hired away Dodger coaches Chuck Dressen and Red Corriden. There was plenty of chirping going on, but Durocher had a bigger issue to deal with when the Dodgers brought Jackie Robinson to training camp with them in 1947. A group of players drew up a petition, protesting the presence of an African-American on their team. Durocher got wind of the revolt and called a midnight meeting to read the riot act to his players. If Robinson was good enough, he would be a Dodger. "I don't care if he's black or yellow or has polka dots or stripes like a zebra," he barked at his players. "He's a great ballplayer, and he's going to help us win games and put money in your pockets."

It was a courageous stance, but Durocher would not get to manage Robinson that year. On the eve of the season, Happy Chandler advised the Dodgers that Durocher was being suspended for a year because he had played fast and loose with the rules of good behavior. It was a series of issues, the commissioner said, all of it bundled under the umbrella phrase "conduct detrimental to baseball." At the core of the problem was the manager's scandalous overnight marriage to Laraine Day while she was still married to someone else. That just is not done in polite circles.

Durocher's relationship with the movie star had caught the attention of the Catholic Youth Organization of Brooklyn. Its director, Vincent J. Powell, decided to withdraw his organization's support of the Dodgers Knothole Gang, a youth program in which the team was deeply invested. Powell sent the Dodgers a scathing letter saying Durocher was undermining the moral training of our youth and represents an example in complete contradiction of our moral teachings.

That was the last straw for Chandler.

The suspension statement was blunt in its language. It began: "Leo Durocher has not measured up to the standards expected or required of managers of our baseball teams. As a result of the accumulation of unpleasant incidents in which he has been involved which the commissioner construes as detrimental to baseball, he is hereby suspended from participating in professional baseball for the 1947 season."

The suspension shocked most people around baseball. It was viewed as using a machete to slice a tomato. Chandler viewed it as a statement that would quiet complaints that he was soft on transgressors. He figured this would be an example that he could be a tough commissioner in the style of Kenesaw Mountain Landis, who had died on Nov. 25, 1944.

Durocher sat out the season, a momentous one in baseball because of the arrival of Jackie Robinson, whose promotion to the Dodgers was announced the day after the manager was benched. A year later, Durocher was back, annoying people and, before too long, dropped by the Dodgers. He simply moved across town to manage the Giants and was in the third base coaches' box when Bobby Thomson hit his pennant-winning home run on Oct. 3, 1951. The victims of that historic homer were Durocher's old pals, the Brooklyn Dodgers.

LEFT: Dickie Kerr was suspended by Commissioner Landis in a contract dispute and mentored Stan Musial, who become one of baseball's greatest hitters. (AP Photo)

BELOW: Mickey Mantle's slugging exploits did not interfere with Commissioner Bowie Kuhn suspending the Yankees star for his work with a casino. (AP Photo)

Willie Mays, also suspended by Commissioner Bowie Kuhn, was reinstated by Commissioner Peter Ueberroth. (AP Photo)

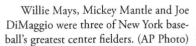

Willie Mays, Mickey Mantle and Joe DiMaggio were three of New York baseball's greatest center fielders. (AP Photo)

Pete Rose finished his career with more hits than anyone in baseball history but was banned for betting on games. (AP Photo)

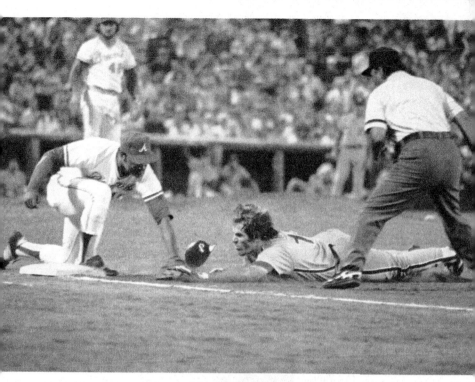

ABOVE: Pete Rose was famous for head-first slides. (AP Photo)

RIGHT: Alex Rodriguez sat out the 2014 season, banned for using steroids and other performance enhancing drugs. (AP Photo)

BELOW: Commissioner Bart Giamatti suspended Pete Rose and then died of a heart attack a week later. (AP Photo)

Commissioner Bud Selig turned down several applications to return to the game by Pete Rose. (AP Photo)

Alex Rodriguez argued for reinstatement before accepting his ban. (AP Photo)

Commissioner Rob Manfred upheld Pete Rose's ban. (AP Photo)

CHAPTER 19

Mexican Jumping Beans

Jorge Pasquel was a Mexican customs broker equipped with plenty of money, an open checkbook and a grand plan to remake baseball in his homeland. Pasquel and his four brothers owned several teams and decided Mexican League baseball needed some new faces, some big stars. To get them, they decided to come to America.

The result was the exodus of 18 players from Major League Baseball, lured south of the border by Pasquel's largesse and creating a large-sized crisis for Commissioner A.B. "Happy" Chandler.

When Kenesaw Mountain Landis died in 1944, the proprietors of baseball decided they wanted a replacement with ties to Washington, D.C. and made Chandler, the former senator and governor of Kentucky, the game's second commissioner. He hardly had settled into the job when the Pasquel problem surfaced.

The Mexican millionaire had already shown a flair for change, integrating the Mexican League by welcoming players of African-American heritage who were barred from playing Major League Baseball. Now Pasquel decided to widen his net. He would offer huge salaries to lure American players to his league. And it worked very quickly, starting in St. Louis, where pitchers Max Lanier and Fred Martin and infielder Lou Klein left almost immediately after hearing Pasquel's offer. The New York Giants lost pitcher Sal Maglie, infielder George Hausmann and outfielder Danny Gardella. Outfielder Luis Olmo and catcher Mickey Owen left Brooklyn for Mexico City. Pasquel was picking off players at an alarming rate. His policy was every player has a price. Meet the price, and you get the player.

Not necessarily. Pasquel is said to have offered Ted Williams a blank check to jump to Mexico. Williams joked that he would like four strikes in every at-bat. "Of course," Pasquel said. "Well," Williams replied, "I won't come anyhow."

Some of Pasquel's other high-profile targets like Joe DiMaggio and Phil Rizzuto also rejected his offers, but he did manage to sign some important players.

Lanier was 6-0 with a 1.93 earned run average when he left the Cardinals for Mexico. He had been a mainstay of three Cardinal championship teams in the 1940s. Vern Stephens of the St. Louis Browns was the defending American League home run champion when he accepted Pasquel's offer. The Mexican businessman even offered Babe Ruth $1 million to become president of the league. Ruth, like the other future Hall of Famers, refused.

Chandler acted quickly. Any player heading for the

Mexican League who did not return by April 1, 1946 would be suspended from Major League Baseball for five years. It was a stiff penalty, and it caused at least one major U-turn when Stephens played two games in Mexico and then went right back to the United States.

Even though other players had better resumes, Pasquel used Owen as his crown jewel, taking the catcher with him to St. Louis on a recruiting trip to try and lure Stan Musial to Mexico. Musial refused, but the Mexican owner had Owen release a statement about how well things were going for expatriate catcher. "I am perfectly happy here," Owen said. "My wife likes Mexico, and we moved into this super modern apartment today, and everything is dandy."

In fact, however, everything wasn't dandy for him. Owen was uncomfortable with the adjustment to a new country where he didn't speak the language, and soon the catcher decided he was going home. Pasquel threatened to sue, but Owen left anyway. He asked for clemency from Major League Baseball, but Chandler refused. Pasquel carried out his threat and soon the catcher with modest ability was caught between the warring leagues. He did not have much support from his colleagues. Stephens, already safely back in Major League Baseball, scoffed at Owen's effort to return. "If they let him come back, anybody can jump contracts anywhere," the shortstop said. Sooner or later, it seemed this matter of the vagabond players would wind up in the courts. And it did.

Cardinals owner Sam Breadon sought a peace treaty with Pasquel. His reward for the effort was a $5,000 fine from Chandler, who had adopted a get-tough stance and was not amused at having one of his owners go off on his own to negotiate.

When Danny Gardella returned to find, like the other players, he had been blacklisted, he turned to the courts. It was a place baseball did not want to be, especially with the game's sacred Reserve Clause at stake. Gardella sued baseball for $100,000, which — under antitrust statutes, which triples damages — would translate to $300,000. The target was baseball's Reserve Clause, which bound players to their teams in perpetuity. The suit included the phrase "restraint of trade," which made Major League Baseball very nervous. Gardella's case was at first dismissed by a federal court judge because of baseball's 1922 antitrust exemption. That ruling was overturned on appeal, and it appeared that the outfielder would have his day in court. Chandler, weary of the battle and wary of what the courts might do, offered amnesty for the Mexican League refugees on July 5, 1949. Peace had been declared.

"Now that the Pasquels had abandoned their foolish raiding, I could afford to be forgiving," the commissioner said. "The suspensions had been in effect for three years. That was a stiff enough penalty. I feel justified in tempering justice with mercy. These players have been ineligible for three years, and nearly all of them have admitted their original mistake."

Most of the players returned to their original teams. Maglie won 18 games for the Giants in 1950, 23 the next year and later pitched a no-hitter for the Dodgers. Lanier had a pair of 11-win seasons for the Cardinals. Fred Martin won 12 games over three years with the Cardinals. Olmo batted .305 in 1949, helping the Dodgers win the pennant. Owen joined the Chicago Cubs for three years and spent a final season with the Boston Red Sox, enjoying modest success.

Gardella, however, found himself unwanted and wound up with Trois Rivières of the Provincial League, a long way from Major League Baseball. Other players dropped their lawsuits. Gardella did not. After enjoying a good season in Canada, batting .286 with 14 home runs and 53 runs batted in, Gardella returned to New York to pursue his lawsuit. Fearing a long, costly court battle, the outfielder reached a settlement. Gardella would receive a $60,000 payoff to drop his suit. He signed with St. Louis, where all the Mexican League trouble had begun, had just one at-bat and never returned to the Major Leagues again. Years later, Curt Flood mounted his own battle against the Reserve Clause and lost in court.

Eventually, however, the players prevailed, and the battle first fought by Danny Gardella was finally won.

CHAPTER 20

Rogue Owners

Owning a baseball team is easy. First, you have to be blessed with a great financial fortune, enough money to indulge in a little fun. Then you need to find a team in economic distress. Put the two together, and in no time you can become a member of an exclusive fraternity and own a stake in Major League Baseball. It's what happens next that can cause trouble.

A perfect example of this was William D. Cox.

Equipped with a degree from Yale University and some excess cash, Cox headed a group that purchased the New York Yankees in 1941. Not those New York Yankees. These Yankees played in the old American Football League. Cox punctuated the purchase by signing Heisman Trophy winner Tom Harmon as the cornerstone of his team. He also quickly became president of the league.

But Cox's timing wasn't great. When World War II

broke out, many players enlisted in the armed forces, and the team and league evaporated. Cox, whose money came from the lumber business, provided pilings for the Panama Canal during the war, but he still wanted to get into sports.

And along came the Philadelphia Phillies.

The team was in deep financial trouble, a consistent also-ran in the National League standings and a money loser at the gate. Owner Gerry Nugent was operating with loans from the league and looking for a buyer. He found one in Bill Veeck, a longtime baseball executive who would go on to become one of baseball's most ingenious promoters. With players in short supply because of the war, Veeck wanted to buy the Phillies and stock the team with players from the Negro Leagues. Commissioner Kenesaw Mountain Landis was not prepared to allow the integration of baseball and vetoed Veeck's plan. Enter Bill Cox.

The price tag for the Phillies in 1943 was $80,000, tip money in today's baseball environment, and Cox then went about reconstructing a team that had finished in last place five straight years. He acquired new players and hired Bucky Harris as manager. Harris had a solid resume that included two trips to the World Series with the Washington Senators. But Cox was a hands-on owner, a former player at Yale who liked to suit up with his team and hang around in the clubhouse. The manager wasn't thrilled with this idea, and the two clashed. Harris' tenure lasted just 92 games. Cox's stay wouldn't be much longer than that.

The day after he was fired, Harris revealed that Cox had been betting on the Phillies, violating one of baseball's cardinal rules. At first, the owner denied the charge, but Landis launched an investigation and discovered that

Harris was right. Cox had been placing bets. The owner stepped down as president of the team, and by the end of the year, he was out of baseball, the first nonplayer to be suspended for life by Landis, law and order commissioner.

It was not the first time a Phillies owner ran afoul of baseball management. Horace Fogel owned the team from 1909–1912. He was invited to leave after arguing out loud that his team was being victimized by the owners. Coupled with the Cox affair — his tenure lasted just eight months — it made the Phillies the only team in Major League Baseball history to have two owners banned from the game. Fred Saigh, however, came close.

Saigh was a successful attorney in St. Louis, often investigating intriguing investments. In 1947, he found one in the city's National League franchise, the Cardinals. Owner Sam Breadon, ailing and frustrated because he was unable to secure a site for a new stadium, put the team on the market. He had set aside a $5 million tax-free fund for the stadium project, and that arrangement became part of Saigh's purchase of the team.

Five years later, Saigh's questionable financial behavior caused him to be indicted on federal charges of evading almost $50,000 in taxes. After pleading no contest to charges, he was sentenced to 15 months in federal prison and released after five months.

Having an ex-convict in their fraternity did not amuse the proprietors of Major League Baseball. Saigh was given an ultimatum. Either sell the team or face a suspension. He chose to sell, although it was difficult at first to find a buyer. Eventually, however, Saigh turned the team over to the prominent St. Louis beer brewery, Anheuser-Busch. The sale price was $3.75 million, for the team Saigh had paid $4 million to buy five years earlier. He was out of baseball, but without the disgrace of suspension that almost certainly would have been imposed had he balked at leaving.

Baseball likes to believe it is an inclusive industry, welcoming one and all under its tent. So the bosses of the game were pleased when Marge Schott came along in 1984, giving the game a female presence in its executive suite. Schott was a prominent Cincinnati businesswoman, owner of a major General Motors dealership and a limited partner in the Reds before assuming controlling interest of the team in 1985.

Then she started talking.

Schott felt no need to hold back. She was an equal opportunity abuser, dropping slurs on almost every minority, praising Adolf Hitler and generally behaving in a way that embarrassed other baseball owners. She would bring her prized St. Bernard, Schottzie, to the ballpark to root for her team. The dog had the run of the place and occasionally relieved himself on the field, an event that did not please the Reds' grounds crew.

She used language not usually found in polite company and didn't care who she insulted, including players on her own team. When she publicly ripped Eric Davis, one of the team's stars, she was slapped with a one-year suspension. It did not alter her behavior. Perhaps the last straw came in 1999, when she observed on a national broadcast interview that, "Hitler was good at the beginning. He just went too far."

That was too far for baseball. Schott was forced to give up day-to-day operation of the team and ordered to stay away from Riverfront Stadium. She got the message and before too long sold the team, just ahead of an almost certain suspension from her baseball partners.

Ted Turner of the Atlanta Braves and Frank McCourt of the Los Angeles Dodgers ran afoul of Major League Baseball and were removed from day-to-day operation of their teams. Turner bought the Braves in 1976 and the next season showed up in the Braves dugout in full uniform to manage the team after firing Dave Bristol. His tenure lasted one day before baseball returned Bristol to his job and suspended Turner, who owned the team until 1996. McCourt used the Dodgers as a personal piggy bank, diverting club funds to maintain a luxurious lifestyle. Baseball frowned on the behavior of both Turner and McCourt and eventually forced both owners to sell their teams. But only one owner has accumulated multiple punishments for his behavior.

When George Steinbrenner headed a syndicate that purchased the New York Yankees for $10 million in 1973, he pledged to be a hands-off owner. The team's operation would be left solely in the hands of his baseball people.

It turned out, though, that Steinbrenner was the Yankees' No. 1 baseball person.

He was brash and bold. He conducted a revolving door of managers, hiring and firing them at a dizzying pace. Billy Martin came through five times, an astounding record. There were feuds with players and feuds with managers and feuds with media. Steinbrenner was front and center, the face of his franchise.

He wanted the Yankees to be baseball's marquee franchise. He spent big in the free agent market, bringing in the game's most prominent players like Reggie Jackson, Catfish

Hunter, Rich Gossage — all future Hall of Famers — and a fistful of others to keep the Yankees at the top. The Jackson signing in 1976 may have been his biggest prize. He signed the slugger as the crown jewel of the first free agent class, a bold statement by the owner that he was back in business, returning to the game after he had been suspended by Commissioner Bowie Kuhn.

In 1974, Steinbrenner pleaded guilty to making illegal political campaign contributions. The penalty from baseball was a two-year suspension. The owner was permitted to return to his team after 15 months, but by 1990, he was in hot water with the baseball authorities again, found to have paid a small-time gambler $40,000 in an effort to get incriminating information on one of his free agent stars, outfielder Dave Winfield, another Hall of Famer. Steinbrenner wanted to avoid making contributions to a Winfield charity, part of the outfielder's free agent contract. Commissioner Fay Vincent imposed a lifetime suspension for cavorting with an unsavory character. Three years later, the ban was lifted, and Steinbrenner celebrated his return by posing for a Sports Illustrated cover riding a white horse and dressed as Napoleon. The man his baseball people called "The Boss" was back in the game, hiring and firing people at a dizzying pace.

He had set a record for owner punishments, was fined multiple times and barred from the game twice. No owner has been suspended since. That doesn't mean another won't be.

CHAPTER 21

The Hit King

For years, each July, in the mapdot village of Cooperstown, New York, birthplace of baseball, a touching tableau has repeated itself.

At one end of Main Street, on a field behind the Hall of Fame museum that celebrates the history of the game, new members are admitted to the shrine with all the appropriate pomp and circumstance. They are surrounded by the greats of the game, gathered to celebrate their achievements.

At the other end of Main Street, the man with the most hits in the history of the game sits alone, signing autographs, shunned by the sport he once dominated.

Pete Rose lives in a baseball purgatory, suspended for betting on baseball but still remembered for the terrific player he was before he fell from fame to infamy.

Every few years, Rose applies for reinstatement, asking forgiveness for sins committed decades ago. And every few years, the request is turned down and the Hit King returns to Cooperstown in July, sitting at the wrong end of Main Street.

In 2016, Commissioner Rob Manfred once again rejected Rose's application for leniency but left a tiny opening, permitting the Cincinnati Reds to admit him to the team's Hall of Fame. The Reds seized the opportunity and honored Rose with a gala weekend in June, retiring his number and celebrating his achievements.

And there were plenty to celebrate.

Rose holds 14 Major League records, with the most significant being his 4,256 hits. He was humbled by the honor the Reds bestowed on him because, at age 75, it was likely to be the only Hall of Fame he will ever reach.

"It means everything," he said. "This is the ultimate for me so far in my baseball career. Everybody I played with is in there. You might as well put me in there, too."

Baseball has been adamant about his lifetime suspension handed down in 1989 after he was found to have bet on games. That is a cardinal sin in the game, with notices posted in every clubhouse warning team personnel about violating it. The Black Sox scandal of 1919 left baseball very sensitive about gambling on games, and Rose took the full brunt of that sensitivity.

For years after the 1989 suspension, Rose denied betting on games. But baseball had tangible proof that he had, indeed, violated that rule. He finally admitted to betting, but it did not change the game's stand regarding his suspension.

Rose said that he is always advised to "reconfigure" his life. It is advice he does not completely understand. Living in Las Vegas, he admits that he bets recreationally, just like many other folks in that city. It is, after all, the town's primary industry. And he sees no reason to alter his lifestyle.

So, the standoff continues. Rose appears comfortable with the situation. Surely, he would like to be honored with the game's other greats in Cooperstown, but for now, the Great American Ballpark in his hometown is a pretty good alternative.

He is a hometown hero, born and bred in Cincinnati, who grew up watching ballgames in Crosley Field, rooting for Reds stars like Ted Kluszewski, Wally Post and Gus Bell, dreaming of one day playing for the team he loved. When he got that chance in 1963, he made the most of it.

During a spring training game against the New York Yankees, he drew a base on balls and charged to first base. Yankees pitcher Whitey Ford watched him and tagged him with the nickname Charlie Hustle. It stuck, because that was the way Rose played the game, an approach punctuated by headfirst slides and collisions.

Long after he became a star, he scored the winning run in the 12th inning of the 1970 All-Star Game, barreling into catcher Ray Fosse, who suffered a broken collarbone and separated shoulder in the collision. There were no apologies. It was just the way Rose played the game.

In 1978, Rose reached the 3,000-hit plateau and then went on a 44-game hitting streak, tying the record set by Wee Willie Keeler. Later, Rose logged time with the Philadelphia Phillies and Montreal Expos before returning to the Reds as player-manager in 1985. On Sept. 11 of that season, against the San Diego Padres, Rose hit a humpback liner to left field for the 4,192nd hit of his career, topping Ty Cobb's record.

At last, Pete Rose was baseball's Hit King.

Rose retired the next season, finishing his career with a .303 batting average and having hit over .300 in 15 of his 24 seasons. He remained as manager of the Reds but ran into trouble in 1988, when he bumped umpire Dave Pallone during an argument and was suspended for 30 days. There was, however, more serious trouble ahead.

Major League Baseball had launched an investigation headed by attorney John Dowd into reports that Rose had been betting on games. In a detailed report, Dowd told the commissioner's office that Rose had bet on 57 games while manager of the Reds. There were reports that he had wagered between $2,000 and $10,000 a day.

Commissioner Bart Giamatti acted swiftly, and on Aug. 24, 1989, he barred Rose for life. Eight days later, the commissioner died of a heart attack. Rose accepted the penalty but never confessed until many years later. He had violated Major League Rule 21, banning anybody associated with baseball from betting on games. If they did, they would face permanent expulsion.

Rose's situation was further complicated in 1990, when he was found guilty of tax evasion and spent five months in a federal penitentiary. Ironically, he was jailed in Marion, Illinois, the hometown of Ray Fosse, the catcher whose career was sent spiraling downward by Rose's 1970 All-Star Game collision.

Although baseball has shunned Rose, it occasionally remembers his contributions to the game. In 1999, he was elected to the game's All-Century team and appeared on the field before Game 2 of the World Series. Applications for reinstatement, however, have been turned down, even after his admission that he had, indeed, bet on baseball.

Years later, controversy still manages to find the man with more hits than anyone else in Major League Baseball history. Early in the 2016 season, Ichiro Suzuki passed Rose's career total. But well over 1,000 of Ichiro's hits came during his career in Japan. Despite that, some media declared the Japanese star the new Hit King with his career total passing Rose's 4,256.

Rose, of course, was not amused by that turn of events. "The next thing you know," he cracked, "they'll be counting his high school hits."

CHAPTER 22

The Steroid King

Baseball has been a roller coaster ride for Alex Rodriguez.

Blessed with enormous natural ability but stalked by the lure of steroids, A-Rod's career was interrupted by the game's longest suspension for using performance-enhancing drugs. He missed an entire season in 2014, after a messy off-season squabble in which he threatened to sue baseball, the players association, the New York Yankees and just about anyone else with whom he could find fault.

There is no denying Rodriguez's talent for playing baseball. That was obvious when the Seattle Mariners made him the No. 1 choice, as an 18-year-old, in baseball's amateur draft in 1993. A year later, he was playing shortstop for the Mariners, just the third 18-year-old to start at the position in the major leagues since 1900.

It was the start of a brilliant but controversial career. In 22 seasons, he accumulated more than 3,000 hits, more than 2,000 runs batted in and 2,000 runs scored. He is a 14-time All-Star with three Most Valuable Player Awards, 10 Silver Sluggers and two Gold Gloves. Just three players, Barry Bonds, Hank Aaron and Babe Ruth have more career home runs.

A-Rod turned heads right from the start, winning his first batting championship in 1996 when he hit. .358, the highest average for a right-handed hitter since Joe DiMaggio batted .381 in 1939 and the third highest ever for a shortstop. He played in the All-Star Game that year, one month before his 21st birthday, becoming the youngest shortstop in the mid-summer game's history. It was the beginning of a brilliant offensive career.

There was always a flare for the dramatic, too, with a record 25 grand slam home runs. In 2007, he became the youngest player to reach 500 home runs. His 3,000th hit was a home run. Only two other players — Derek Jeter and Wade Boggs — have done that.

And yet, there have been troubling flaws in A-Rod's game.

He left the Mariners in 2001, signing the richest contract in baseball history, a $252 million deal with the Texas Rangers. It was during those years that he said the pressures of that contract forced him to seek an edge, and that was when he first gave into the demons of drugs. He won his first MVP award in 2003 and the next year was traded to the New York Yankees where, with Jeter a fixture at shortstop, A-Rod agreed to play third base. Rodriguez arrived in New York with an impressive resume, and he added to it with the Yankees. He had set a record for home runs by a shortstop with 57 in 2002 and then set a record for home runs by a third baseman with 52 in 2007. He soared past Willie Mays' 660 home runs to take fourth place on the all-time list.

There were two more MVP awards in his first four years in New York, but there was also a troubling tendency to flop badly in the postseason, when his average was below .200. Then, in 2007, he opted out of his contract, choosing to announce his decision in the middle of a World Series game between Boston and Colorado. It was an example of Rodriguez upstaging his sport, something baseball did not appreciate.

The Yankees re-signed him to a 10-year, $275 million contract, and he led New York to a World Series championship in 2009. It was a turnaround postseason, too, when he batted .365 with six home runs in 15 games. It was that year, however, that he confessed to his steroid history with Texas after denying it in a national television interview two years earlier. He called himself "stupid and naive" for getting involved with steroids.

Hip surgery sidelined Rodriguez at the start of the 2009 season. When he returned in May, he hit a home run on the first pitch of his first at-bat, again displaying that flair for the dramatic. He again had hip surgery in 2013, but there was more drug trouble to come. His name surfaced as part of a Biogenesis scandal at a time when A-Rod was quarreling with the Yankees over his rehabilitation from his second hip surgery. He returned to the Yankees lineup on Aug. 5, the same day baseball announced the Biogenesis penalties, and Rodriguez was suspended for 211 games, the remainder of the 2013 season and all of 2014. He appealed and was allowed to continue playing. Finally, an arbitrator reduced the suspension to 162 games, the full 2014 season.

Baseball charged him with the use of multiple PEDs, including testosterone and human growth hormones "over the course of multiple years," and trying to interfere with baseball's investigation. It was an ugly time for Rodriguez. After first fighting the suspension with lawsuits, A-Rod backed off and accepted the suspension.

At age 38, it could have been the end of the road for him. But after settling his quarrels with the Yankees, Rodriguez went about proving the critics wrong for much of the 2015 season. Limited to designated hitter status, Rodriguez had a big year. He finished the season with 33 home runs, leading the Yankees in home runs, on-base percentage and slugging percentage. But he struggled in the final two months of the season, batting just .191 after Aug. 1 with 59 strikeouts in 183 at-bats. It was a bad sign for a player his age.

When Rodriguez slumped at the start of the 2016 season, he found himself benched and an afterthought in the Yankees lineup he once dominated. There were calls for him to be released, for the Yankees to pay off the last year of his contract and show him the door. At age 41, he seemed done. In August, he agreed to walk away from playing and became a special assistant to co-owner Hal Steinbrenner. His role was to tutor younger players in the Yankees farm system, but there was speculation that he might return to the game to pursue the four home runs he needed to reach 700 for his career.

CHAPTER 23

They Suspended Who?

The news hit baseball like a thunderclap.

Willie Mays was suspended by Commissioner Bowie Kuhn in 1979, just months after he was inducted into the Hall of Fame. And then, just to prove he was serious about the matter, Kuhn followed that up by suspending Mickey Mantle in 1983.

Mays and Mantle are two of the greatest center fielders in baseball history. When he was suspended, Mays' resume included 660 home runs, the third most in history at that time. Mantle was the last American League Triple Crown winner. Both were icons of the game. And, just like that, the commissioner threw them out.

In the Deadball Era, scores of players were suspended, some for life, for gambling, fixing games, taking bribes or offering them and the like. In the modern era, players were suspended for taking steroids and other performance-enhancing drugs.

Mays and Mantle did neither. Their violation was taking glad-hand jobs with Atlantic City casinos, playing golf or just hanging out and gabbing with important customers. And for this, Kuhn barred them from baseball.

To say the penalties were shockers would be an understatement. Kuhn felt he was protecting the integrity of the game, much the way Judge Kenesaw Mountain Landis did when he swept out dozens of players after becoming commissioner in 1920. Kuhn had been down this road before, suspending Detroit pitching star Denny McLain for alleged involvement with a Michigan gambling ring. McLain felt the suspension hammer three times in 1970, believed to be a single season record. And when Ferguson Jenkins showed up at a Toronto airport with a variety of drugs and was arrested in 1980, Kuhn suspended him, too.

McLain's post-baseball career was pockmarked with trouble, including two jail sentences for racketeering, embezzlement, drug possession and the theft of pension funds from a company he owned. Jenkins, whose suspension lasted two weeks before an arbitrator set it aside, wound up in the Hall of Fame, alongside Mays and Mantle.

McLain was baseball's last 30-game winner, a star for sure. Jenkins was one of baseball's best pitchers. But they were not in the class of Mays and Mantle, who were baseball royalty, equipped with some of the best portfolios of any players in the history of the game. Kuhn's decision to ban them seemed over the top, certainly considering his reason.

When Mays signed a 10-year deal with Bally's International as a goodwill ambassador, Kuhn warned him that the deal was "inconsistent" with baseball's best interests. When Mays went ahead and signed the $100,000 deal, twice what he was being paid by the New York Mets, the commissioner brought down the suspension hammer.

Mays was stunned by the decision. "I've been a model for baseball for 22 years, " he said. "But now I have to think primarily of my family."

Three years later, the scenario was repeated. Mantle agreed to work for the Claridge Hotel and Casino in Atlantic City, and Kuhn suspended him. The message was the same. "Baseball and casino employment are inconsistent," the commissioner said.

Mantle, in his "aw shucks" style, shrugged off the decision. "I wasn't doing that much in baseball anyway," he said. "I don't have any hard feelings toward the commissioner. But he should understand that I'm not going to be standing in front of the hotel saying, 'Come in and gamble.'"

Peter Ueberroth understood that.

In the first days after he succeeded Kuhn as commissioner, Ueberroth reinstated both Mays and Mantle to good standing within the baseball community.

"I am bringing back two players who are more a part of baseball than anyone else," the new commissioner said.

It was a brilliant public relations move, celebrated throughout the industry and the country. Mays and Mantle were understandably thrilled. "This is a happy occasion for Mickey and me to have that word 'ban' lifted," Mays said. "I don't think I did anything wrong to leave baseball. It's a good feeling to know I can still make a living and go back to baseball."

Mantle echoed those feelings.

"Like Willie, I know we never did anything wrong," he said. "Mr. Kuhn felt he did the right thing. He warned me he would ban me, so I took the job with my eyes wide open. I know it was hard for Mr. Ueberroth to do this, but he felt it had to be done."

Kuhn, too, understood the new commissioner's decision. "I disagree with his decision, and I make no bones about it," Kuhn said. "I still would not reverse what I did."

That said, Kuhn admitted that Mays and Mantle had always been good citizens and positive representatives for baseball.

After the suspensions were lifted, Mays and Mantle made promotional appearances for baseball, goodwill ambassadors for the game they dominated for so long. And they continued to play golf with casino customers.

CHAPTER 24

The Moderns

In 2017, the minimum salary for a Major League Baseball player was $535,000. That means the 25th man on the roster made over a half million dollars. This salary inflation has been a function of free agency and eliminated the threat of bribes and fixed games that infiltrated the game a century ago and led to an epidemic of players being banned from baseball.

That does not mean, however, that modern players have avoided trouble with the commissioner's office. Dozens of players have been suspended for baseball's newest scourge—drugs.

Perhaps the most notorious violator was relief pitcher Steve Howe, who was suspended from baseball for alcohol and drug issues seven times in a 17-year career. Howe had been Rookie of the Year in 1980 and saved the World Series clinching game for the Los Angeles Dodgers in 1981. But he was haunted throughout his career by substance abuse problems. One of his suspensions was a lifetime sentence, but it was overturned on appeal. Howe died in a truck accident in 2006, and an autopsy revealed methamphetamine in his system.

Rafael Palmeiro finished his 20-year career with 569 home runs and 3,020 hits, one of just five players to reach both of those offensive thresholds. He was implicated as a drug abuser in a tell-all book by Jose Canseco and testified before Congress, vigorously denying the charge, famously pointing his finger at the panel of lawmakers for emphasis. Then, on Aug. 1, 2005, he was suspended for 10 days after failing a drug test.

Ordinarily, 500 home runs or 3,000 hits are automatic tickets to the Hall of Fame, but in his second year of eligibility, Palmeiro failed to get 5 percent of the votes to maintain his name on the ballot and is no longer eligible for election by the Baseball Writers Association of America.

In 1998, baseball was electrified by the long ball heroics of Mark McGwire, who broke Roger Maris' single season record of 61 home runs, finishing with 70. Years later, McGwire admitted he had been using performance-enhancing drugs and that his home run total had been helped by artificial additives.

McGwire was never suspended because the proprietors of the game chose to look the other way during what has become known as the steroid era. That changed when the Major League Players Association and the commissioner's office agreed to new rules with periodic testing to make sure players were not using PEDs.

In 2014, baseball toughened the penalty for violating

the drug policy. Now players are banned 80 games for the first violation, 162 games for the second and receive a lifetime ban for a third violation. The lifetime ban allows players to apply for reinstatement after one year and, if approved, to return to baseball one year after that.

Even though the players know they will be tested periodically, some continue to violate the rules and wind up sidelined. Included in the casualties in the first half of the 2016 season were the defending National League batting champion, who sat out 80 games; a veteran player who came back from an earlier suspension and then was hit with a 162-game ban; and a relief pitcher who tested positive for a third time and received a lifetime ban.

Each of the players expressed shock and remorse over their suspensions. Perhaps the saddest of all was Marlon Byrd, who had been suspended for 50 games in 2012 and battled his way back to the majors, becoming a productive player for the Mets. He then moved to Pittsburgh, Philadelphia, Cincinnati and San Francisco and did well at every stop. At age 38, he signed with Cleveland and then, two months into the season, was suspended for drugs again, this time for a full season, 162 games. This, he admitted, effectively finished his career, and he told teammates he never wanted it to end this way.

In contrast to Byrd, a journeyman veteran who played for 10 teams over 13 years, Dee Gordon of the Miami Marlins was one of baseball's bright young stars. A two-time All-Star, he led the National League with a .333 batting average, 205 hits and 58 stolen bases in 2015 and was the catalyst at the top of the Marlins' lineup. He signed a $50 million contract extension in the off-season.

And then he tested positive for steroids.

Gordon said he had always been careful with supplements, avoiding any substance on baseball's banned list. One mistake, however, cost him half of the 2016 season.

Jenrry Mejia's penalty was the stiffest — a lifetime ban after failing a drug test for the third time. He tested positive for the first time in April 2015. Sidelined for 80 games, he returned in July, apologized to his teammates and after pitching in just seven games, found himself suspended again, this time for 162 games. That suspension was to end in July 2016, and the Mets signed him to a contract, hoping he would bolster their bullpen in mid-season. Then came the third failed test, and the Dominican pitcher became the first player banned for life since Pete Rose in 1989.

Others suspended included Abraham Almonte of Cleveland, Daniel Stumpf of Philadelphia, Chris Colabello of Toronto, Josh Ravin of the Los Angeles Dodgers and Raul Mondesi Jr. of Kansas City. Each sat out 80 games except Mondesi, whose ban was reduced on appeal from 80 games to 50 because he had used an over-the-counter medication he purchased in the Dominican Republic.

Drug violations aren't baseball's only problem. After ugly domestic abuse violations surfaced in other sports, baseball adopted a policy and quickly found two high-profile players had violated it.

One day apart at the end of October 2015, infielder Jose Reyes and relief pitcher Aroldis Chapman got in trouble with legal authorities for domestic abuse. Reyes was arrested in Hawaii after a physical altercation with his wife, and Chapman got in trouble in Florida for a similar issue as well as firing a gun six times in his garage.

Both players were suspended. Reyes sat out 52 games before being released by the Colorado Rockies and signing with the New York Mets. Chapman, equipped with a 100-mile-per-hour fastball, was traded by Cincinnati to the New York Yankees and then suspended for 30 games. At the trade deadline, Chapman was sent to the Chicago Cubs and after they won the World Series in 2016, returned to the Yankess as a free agent.

Both players offered apologies for their mistakes and hoped to put the problems behind them and continue with what had been productive major league careers. At least they had a chance to come back after their troubles.

Scores of others, banned and placed on baseball's blacklist, never got that chance.

CHAPTER 25

And Then A General Manager, Too

Most of the individuals suspended or banned from baseball have been players, with an occasional owner, umpire or even a club physician included in the mix. Then, in the final weeks of the 2016 season, they were joined by new member — a general manager.

A.J. Preller was named to run the front office of the San Diego Padres in August 2014, a graduate of Cornell University and one of the latest Ivy League–educated executives who have taken over high-profile jobs running Major League Baseball clubs.

Preller, 36 at the time, was considered one of the game's brightest young executives, but his fall from grace occurred when it was discovered that the Padres maintained two sets of medical records for their players, one available for potential trade partners to examine, the other a private one for club use only. The reports in the two sets did not always agree. There was, for example, the matter of pitcher Drew Pomeranz.

It turned out, the Padres had withheld some crucial information on Pomeranz, much the way they had when they traded pitcher Colin Rea to the Miami Marlins earlier in the 2016 season. Rea's first start for the Marlins lasted four innings before his arm gave out. The trade was rescinded and the pitcher may be headed for Tommy John surgery.

Then Pomeranz, who was 8-7 with a 2.47 earned run average for the Padres, was traded to Boston for 18-year-old pitching prospect Anderson Espinoza. It sounded like a steal for the Red Sox, who were getting an established major leaguer for a teenaged prospect. But it turned out that the medical report the Red Sox examined before making the deal did not disclose everything it should have about the pitcher they were getting. The public report left out the fact that Pomeranz had been taking an oral medication for a sore elbow for weeks before the trade was completed. The elbow flared up in Boston where he went 3-5 with a 4.62 ERA. Major League Baseball was not amused with the subterfuge and in an unprecedented move, ordered Preller suspended for 30 days without pay. It was not his first scrape with baseball authorities.

Preller was on baseball's fast track even while he was in college, working as a summer intern for the Philadelphia Phillies. He also had jobs with the Los Angeles Dodgers and Major League Baseball before being hired in 2004 by the Texas Rangers as director of international scouting. His boss with the Rangers was Jon Daniels, who, coincidently, happened to be Preller's fraternity brother and roommate at Cornell. Preller eventually became the Rangers' assistant general manager and was credited with building a strong farm system for the team.

It was during his stint with Texas that Preller first got in trouble with baseball authorities. He allegedly negotiated with an agent to sign pitcher Rafael de Paula, who had been suspended for lying about his age. He also worked out and signed outfielder Julio Beras, claiming he was 17. There was suspicion that Beras was 16 at the time and ineligible to be signed for several months under terms of the Collective Bargaining Agreement.

The original suspension was reported to be for three months but was reduced to one month on appeal. Still, it marked Preller as someone who operated on the fringe of the rules, a fact that the Padres chose to ignore when they signed him to a five-year contract as their general manager.

When he was hired, Preller talked about a front office that would be cutting-edge in its approach. He said he wanted a "next wave" operation that was "ahead of the curve."

"You constantly have to hit on ideas that give you a competitive advantage and, when the competition catches up, hopefully hit on the next idea to take us where we need to get to," he said.

In San Diego, he became a wheeler-dealer, importing high-profile players like pitchers James Shields and Craig Kimbrel and outfielders Matt Kemp and Justin Upton for short stays before shuffling them off to other teams. He also fired manager Bud Black, who had been on the job for nine years.

The plan got off to a slow start with the Padres posting records of 74-88 and 68-94 in Preller's first two full seasons on the job. In the middle of his second full season came the Pomeranz affair and the suspension, which left the Padres with a black eye in the industry and Preller appropriately contrite.

"I accept full responsibility for issues related to the oversight of our medical administration and record keeping," he said in a prepared statement. "I want to emphasize that there was no malicious intent on the part of me or anyone on my staff to conceal information or disregard MLB's recommended guidelines. This has been a learning process for me. I will serve my punishment and look forward to being back on the job in 30 days."

In another joint statement, Padres executive chairman Ron Fowler, managing partner Peter Seidler and president and chief executive officer Mike Dee called the episode "unintentional but inexcusable," and pledged to remedy the situation in the team's maintenance of medical records. Dee, who hired Preller, was dismissed shortly before the GM's suspension ended.

"I think the penalty speaks for itself," commissioner Rob Manfred said of Preller's suspension. "I think clubs in general fully disclose medical records consistent with a long-standing practice in baseball. I'm confident clubs adhere to those guidelines."

In this case, however, the Padres did not, and it resulted in Preller joining the community of those who have been banned by baseball.

Afterword

Outlaws in baseball are as old as the game itself, and given the frailties of man are likely to keep cropping up for as long as the sport is played. As Hal Bock details so vividly, the intersection of temptation and triumph, rogues and riches, has led to a series of scandals that seem never-ending in the game's century-and-a-half timeline.

The centennial of baseball's low point is upcoming: the fixed World Series of 1919, an event so seismic that it is part of the nation's culture. Hyman Roth, the fictional Jewish mobster in "The Godfather Part II" is born Hyman Suchowsky but when asked whom he most admires cites Arnold Rothstein, the gambler at the center of the Series fix, and is thus renamed.

As Major League Baseball has evolved from a daytime pastime in 16 ballparks from St. Louis on east to a nation-wide multibillion-dollar industry and media and digital conglomerate with aspirations of global dominance, gambling-related transgressions have faded. Pete Rose's lifetime ban for betting on Cincinnati to win while managing his hometown Reds stands out as the supreme sin since World War II, and the establishment (commissioners Fay Vincent, Bud Selig and Rob Manfred, and Hall of Fame chair Jane Forbes Clark) have held firm in his exclusion from baseball society.

Others no doubt will fall, and when their tribulations are recounted, Hal's book will be an invaluable resource for future historians.

—Ron Blum, AP Baseball Writer

Lifetime Bans from Baseball

The following is a list of lifetime bans imposed since 1920 and compiled by John Thorn, official historian of Major League Baseball:

Joe Jackson, **Buck Weaver**, **Eddie Cicotte**, **Lefty Williams**, **Happy Felsch**, **Fred McMullin**, **Swede Risberg** and **Chick Gandil**: Implicated in the 1919 Chicago Black Sox World Series scandal.

Joe Gedeon: Second baseman of the St. Louis Browns who, like Weaver, sat in on a meeting with gamblers, had "guilty knowledge" and failed to share it with authorities.

Gene Paulette: Banished by Kenesaw Mountain Landis for his association with St. Louis gamblers in 1919, even though he had played a complete 1920 season.

Benny Kauff: Arrested for auto theft but acquitted at trial and was banned anyway as he was, in Landis' words, "no longer a fit companion for other ballplayers."

Lee Magee: Released by Chicago, then — after questioning at a trial over his disputed back salary elicited evidence of his gambling involvements — banned by Landis.

Heinie Zimmerman: Banned in 1921 for encouraging his teammates to fix games; he had been blacklisted since 1919.

Heinie Groh: Banned after rejecting Cincinnati's salary offer; Landis' condition for reinstatement was that he could return to play for the Reds only; two days after the ban, Groh did.

Ray Fisher: Declined a Reds' pay cut and sat out the season until hired by the University of Michigan to coach its baseball team. Landis banned him from organized baseball for violating the Reserve Clause, but Fisher never returned. The ban was overturned by Bowie Kuhn in 1980.

Dickie Kerr: A "Clean Sox" hero of the 1919 World Series, was banned after he played in an outlaw league in 1922 rather than accept the ChiSox pay offer. Thus violating the Reserve Clause, Kerr was banned. Landis reinstated him in 1925, and he pitched for Chicago again.

Jim "Hippo" Vaughn: Played a semipro game under an assumed name while under contract to the Cubs in 1921. His case was referred to Landis, who banned Vaughn for the rest of the season. When he signed a three-year contract with the Beloit Fairies, a semipro team, his status as a contract jumper was solidified. Although Landis permitted his reinstatement in 1931, Vaughn failed in his attempt to make the Cubs' squad.

Shufflin' Phil Douglas: Player for the Giants, angry with John McGraw, got drunk and sent a letter to a friend on the Cardinals suggesting that he would "disappear" when the club came to St. Louis. Landis banned him for life.

Jimmy O'Connell: A second-year player with the Giants in 1924, offered a bribe to Heinie Sand of the Phils; perhaps he was the naive victim of a joke perpetrated by Giants coach **Cozy Dolan**. Landis banned both. John McGraw's involvement has long been surmised but never proven.

Cletus Elwood "Boots" Poffenberger: Supended by Landis at the request of the Brooklyn Dodgers in 1939 after he declined to report to Montreal. He then was reinstated at Brooklyn's request in early 1940 so that his contract could be sold to Nashville of the Southern Association, for whom he won 26 games. He pitched for several other clubs in the minors but never returned to the majors.

William Cox: Phillies' owner, was banned for betting on baseball games and forced to sell his franchise. Occurring in 1943, this was Landis' last banishment. (In 1953, St. Louis owner Fred Saigh was forced to divest his control of the Cardinals when he began a fifteen-month sentence for tax evasion; that paved the way for Saigh's sale of the team to Anheuser-Busch. Saigh was not formally banned, however.)

Sal Maglie, Max Lanier, Ace Adams, Danny Gardella, Luis Olmo and Others: Banned for five years after jumping to the Mexican League in 1946. Happy

Chandler rescinded many of these bans, however, in settlement of lawsuits.

Ferguson Jenkins: After being arrested in Toronto for possessing cocaine in August 1980, was banned two weeks later by Commissioner Bowie Kuhn. An arbitrator overturned the ban in September 1980.

Mickey Mantle and **Willie Mays**: Banned by Kuhn in 1983 because they worked as greeters at an Atlantic City casino. Commissioner Peter Ueberroth reinstated both in 1985.

Pete Rose: Banned by Commissioner Bart Giamatti in 1989. Several appeals have been unsuccessful, most recently in 2015.

George Steinbrenner: Banned by Commissioner Fay Vincent in 1990, who reinstated him two years later.

Steve Howe: After six prior drug suspensions, was banned on the same day that Vincent reinstated Steinbrenner. The ban was overturned by an arbitrator in November 1992.

Marge Schott: Cincinnati Reds owner that was banned by Bud Selig in 1996 for bringing Major League Baseball into disrepute by repeatedly uttering racial, ethnic and homophobic slurs. She was reinstated in 1998.

Jenrry Mejia: Mets pitcher, received a permanent suspension from organized baseball on February 12, 2016, following a third failed drug test.

Baseball Rules For Misconduct And Substance Abuse

Note: The Collective Bargaining Agreement (CBA) signed in December 2016 increased the number of in-season random tests from 3,200 to 4,800. In addition, every player is to be tested at least once every off-season with increased penalties for violations in the form of forfeited service time and lost pay.

The new CBA also banned smokeless tobacco for all players who reach the Major Leagues in 2017.

MAJOR LEAGUE RULE 21
MISCONDUCT

(a) MISCONDUCT IN PLAYING BASEBALL. Any

player or person connected with a club who shall promise or agree to lose, or to attempt to lose, or to fail to give his best efforts towards the winning of any baseball game with which he is or may be in any way concerned; or who shall intentionally fail to give his best efforts towards the winning of any such baseball game, or who shall solicit or attempt to induce any player or person connected with a club to lose, or attempt to lose, or to fail to give his best efforts towards the winning of any baseball game with which such other player or person is or may be in any way connected; or who, being solicited by any person, shall fail to inform his Major League President and the Commissioner.

(b) GIFT FOR DEFEATING COMPETING CLUB. Any player or person connected with a club who shall offer or give any gift or reward to a player or person connected with another club for services rendered or supposed to be or to have been rendered in defeating or attempting to defeat a competing club, and any player or person connected with a club who shall solicit or accept from a player connected with another club any gifts or reward for any such services rendered, or supposed to have been rendered, or who having been offered any such gift or reward, shall fail to inform his League President or the Commissioner immediately of such offer, and of all facts and circumstances therewith, shall be declared ineligible for not less than three (3) years.

(c) GIFTS TO UMPIRES. Any player or person connected with a club, who shall give, or offer to give, any gift or reward to an umpire for services rendered, or supposed to be or to have been rendered, in defeating or attempting to defeat a competing club, or for the umpire's decision on anything connected with the playing of a baseball game;

and any umpire who shall render, or promise or agree to render, any such decision otherwise than on its merits, or who shall solicit or accept such gifts or reward, or having been solicited to render any such decision otherwise than on its merits, shall fail to inform the League President or the Commissioner immediately of such offer or solicitation, and all facts and circumstances therewith, shall be declared permanently ineligible.

(d) BETTING ON BALL GAMES. Any player, umpire, or club official or employee, who shall bet any sum whatsoever upon any baseball game in connection with which the bettor has no duty to perform shall be declared ineligible for one year.

Any player, umpire, or club or league official or employee, who shall bet any sum whatsoever upon any baseball game in connection with which the bettor has a duty to perform shall be declared permanently ineligible.

(e) VIOLENCE OR MISCONDUCT IN INTERLEAGUE GAMES. In case of any physical attack or other violence upon an umpire by a player, or by an umpire upon a player, or of other misconduct by an umpire or a player, during or in connection with any interleague Major League game or any exhibition game of a Major League Club with a club or team not a member of the same league, the Commissioner shall impose upon the offender or offenders such fine, suspension, ineligibility or other penalty, as the facts may warrant in the judgement of the Commissioner.

(f) OTHER MISCONDUCT. Nothing herein contained shall be construed as exclusively defining or otherwise limiting acts, transactions, practices or conduct not to be in the best interests of Baseball; and any and all other acts, transactions, practices or conduct not to be in the best interests of Baseball are prohibited and shall be subject to such penalties, including permanent ineligibility, as the facts in the particular case may warrant.

(g) RULE TO BE KEPT POSTED. A printed copy of this Rule shall be kept posted in each clubhouse.

SUBSTANCE ABUSE RULES

- The number of in-season random urine collections will more than double beginning in the 2014 season (from 1,400 to 3,200), which are in addition to the mandatory urine collections that every player is subjected to both during Spring Training and the Championship Season. This represents the largest increase in testing frequency in the program's history.
- Blood collections for HGH detection — which remains the most significant HGH blood testing program of its kind in American professional sports — will increase to 400 random collections per year, in addition to the 1,200 mandatory collections conducted during Spring Training.
- A first-time performance-enhancing substance violation of the Joint Drug Program will now result in an unpaid 80-game suspension, increased from 50 games. A player's second violation will result in an unpaid 162-game suspension (and a loss of 183 days of pay), increased from 100 games. A third violation will result in a permanent suspension from baseball.
- A player who is suspended for a violation involving a

performance-enhancing substance will be ineligible to participate in the postseason and will not be eligible for an automatic share of the player's pool provided to players on clubs who participate in the postseason. (Such players are already ineligible to participate in the All-Star Game.)

- Every player whose suspension for a performance-enhancing substance is upheld will be subject to six additional unannounced urine collections, and three additional unannounced blood collections, during every subsequent year of his entire career.

- Carbon Isotope Ratio Mass Spectrometry (IRMS) will be randomly performed on at least one specimen from every player in addition to any IRMS test that the laboratory conducts as a result of the parties' longitudinal profiling program (which was implemented prior to the 2013 season) and the World Anti-Doping Agency (WADA) guidelines for conducting IRMS.

- The parties established a program in which players will have year-round access to supplements that will not cause a positive test result and which will improve home and visiting weight rooms.

- The parties provided the arbitration panel with the ability to reduce a player's discipline (subject to certain limitations) for the use of certain types of performance-enhancing substances if the player proves at a hearing that the use was not intended to enhance performance.

- The parties added DHEA to the list of banned substances and enhanced the confidentiality provisions of the program.

References

CHAPTER 5
- Sam Crawford quote: "Cobb wasn't easy to get along with ..." "The Glory of Their Times" By Lawrence Ritter

CHAPTER 6
- Benny Kauff quote: "I'll make them all forget Cobb" SABR Biographical Project
- Benny Kauff quote: "They'll have to put up screens to protect the fans" SABR Biographical Project
- John McGraw quote: "Kauff is innocent" SABR Biographical Project
- Judge Landis quote: "Benny Kauff's involvement ..."' SABR Biographical Project

CHAPTER 8
- Heinie Zimmerman quote: "You poor fish ..." SABR Biographical Project

CHAPTER 9
- Judge Landis quote: "Regardless of the outcome of juries …" Biographical Encyclopedia of Baseball
- Gabby Hartnett quote: "If I visit his place of business …" Wikipedia

CHAPTER 10
- Judge Landis quote: "Regardless of the outcome …" Biographical Encyclopedia of Baseball

CHAPTER 11
- Judge Landis quote: "No player who sits in conference …" Biographical Encyclopedia of Baseball
- Judge Landis quote: "Birds of a feather …" "The Commissioners" By Jerome Holtzman
- Judge Landis quote: "Men associating with gamblers and crooks …" "The Commissioners" By Jerome Holtzman

CHAPTER 17
- Phil Douglas quote: "I want to leave here, but I want some inducement" "The Commissioners" By Jerome Holtzman; SABR Biographical Project

CHAPTER 18
- George Magerkurth quote: "I'm going to reach down and bite your head off" Biographical Encyclopedia of Baseball
- Leo Durocher quote: "I don't care if he's black or yellow or has polka dot or stripes like a zebra" Biographical Encyclopedia of Baseball

- Happy Chandler quote: "Leo Durocher has not measured up to standards ..." "The Commissioners" By Jerome Holtzman

CHAPTER 19
- Mickey Owen quote: "I am perfectly happy here ..." Baseball Almanac
- Happy Chandler quote: "Now that the Pasquels have abandoned ..." National Pastime Museum

CHAPTER 20
- Marge Schott quote: "Hitler was good at the beginning ..." Brainy Quote homepage

CHAPTER 21
- Pete Rose quote: "It means everything ..." Associated Press
- Pete Rose quote: "The next thing you know ..." USA Today

CHAPTER 23
- Willie Mays quote: "I've been a model for baseball ..." Associated Press
- Bowie Kuhn quote: "Baseball and casino employment ..." Associated Press
- Mickey Mantle quote: "I wasn't doing much in baseball anyway" Associated Press
- Peter Ueberroth quote: "I am bring back two players ..." Associated Press
- Willie Mays quote: "This is a happy occasion ..." Associated Press

- Mickey Mantle quote: "Like Willie, I knew ..." Associated Press
- Bowie Kuhn quote: "I disagree with the decision ..." Associated Press

Acknowledgments

History books like this one require considerable research. I was fortunate to have terrific resources for that, such as "The Biographical Encyclopedia of Baseball," "The Commissioners" by Jerome Holtzman, "Great Baseball Feats, Facts & Firsts" by David Nemec, "The History of National League Baseball" by Glenn Dickey, "The Joe Williams Baseball Reader" and "The Society for American Baseball Research Biographical Project." Thanks, too, to old friend Bob Rosen of Elias Sports Bureau for fact checking.

• • •

The Associated Press would like to thank Hal Bock, John Thorn, Peter Costanzo, Chris Sullivan, Valerie Komor, Francesca Pitaro, Paul Colford, Lauren Easton, Mike Bowser, Ron Blum and the entire team at Diversion Books.

HAL BOCK was an award-winning sports writer and columnist at The Associated Press for 40 years, covering every major event on the sports calendar, including 30 World Series, 30 Super Bowls and 11 Olympic Games. He has written scores of magazine articles and is the author of 16 books, including the recently published "The Last Chicago Cubs Dynasty Before the Curse" as well as narratives for "The Complete Encyclopedia of Ice Hockey," "The Associated Press Pictorial History of Baseball" and "Willard Mullin's Golden Age of Baseball Drawings." He has also taught journalism at St. John's University and Long Island University. He lives in East Williston, New York with his wife, a retired psychologist, and their cat, a rescued stray.

CPSIA information can be obtained
at www.ICGtesting.com
Printed in the USA
BVOW06s1356140517
484109BV00017B/247/P

9 781635 760316